Famous Clergy

Profiles of Jeremy Taylor, George Walker, Jonathan Swift, Thomas Percy, Richard Mant, William Alexander and William Shaw Kerr

S.E. Long

The image on the front cover is from the Charles Shannon Memorial Window in St. Paul's Parish Church, Lisburn, Co. Antrim. It depicts King Solomon and Hiram at the building of the Temple. It was dedicated by Rev. Canon Dr. Kenneth W. Cochrane on 18th October 1998.

Slieve Croob Press
Northern Ireland

First published in 2013 by Slieve Croob, available in the United Kingdom and Republic of Ireland from Slieve Croob Press, and worldwide through the Internet.

Copyright © 2013 S.E. Long

ISBN: 978-1-291-40655-9

Printed and bound in the United Kingdom of Great Britain and Northern Ireland.

Contents

The collaboration of Rev. Stanley Gamble, colleague and friend in the publication of this book is thankfully acknowledged.

S.E. Long

Introduction

The seven churchmen profiled here had in their own times a considerable influence on the Church of Ireland. While their contributions were many and varied, each of them stamped something of his personality on the church. It is of more than passing interest that five of them were bishops, one was about to become a bishop and the ambition of the other was to be a bishop. If this says anything it is that in Irish Anglicanism bishops were not only able academics and administrators but their status gave them privileges, opportunities and responsibilities which in the case of these bishops were used positively and sometimes provocatively. The fact that the work of several of the seven remains important to the church, and that a few of them continue to the world at large as valuable interpreters of what is important to humanity, is evidence not just of the durability of it and them but of a perennial relevance.

The quality common to all of them was their devotion to their own church while most of them had no difficulty in sharing theological perceptions and sociological attitudes with those of other churches. Kerr differed to an extent in his strong emphasis on ecumenism. His efforts to forge an institutional link between the Presbyterian Church and the Church of Ireland, aborted largely by J.A.F.Gregg, could have changed the size and shape of denominationalism in Ireland. The support he had in both churches has not been available to ecumenists since that time. An observer of the Irish religious scene now could well conclude that division is more indelibilised than ever. The friendly sharing in causes of mutual concern by church leaders does nothing consequentially to change that situation.

The authority and influence of the episcopate have been diminished and especially in the last quarter century. The autocratic rule of bishops has gone in Irish Anglicanism. The bishop today has such informal relationships with his clergy and people they ensure that he is in close contact with them, closer than appears to have been the case in other days. The clergyman elected to the episcopate need not be warned now that as a bishop he will never be short of a meal and never be told the truth. Many things have contributed to the present position. One of them must be the determination of parish clergy and people to make their own decisions in consultation with the bishop and always after agreement with the diocesan council or one of its committees. The premier place of the General Synod in Irish Anglicanism has become a reality with its strong lay input into all its discussions, debates and decisions. The leadership role of the Bishops and the House of Bishops is acknowledged as is their considerable contributions to the workings of General Synod and its committees and agencies. Bishops are chairmen by appointment of the Bench of these elected representative groups.

The office of a bishop has become more markedly that of the Father in God who encourages, inspires, leads and guides those in his care. They will often do as he suggests while retaining their right to do what they think is best for them. This self confidence is a reason for the comparative church strength in a largely secularised society. It has made the Church of Ireland one of the most democratic in Anglicanism with clergy and people together committed to the growth and maintenance of their church. It could be that these seven churchmen have in their lives emphasised the place and purpose of leadership in the church. Each of them accepted the duties, responsibilities and opportunities of leadership and selflessly spent himself in the pursuit of causes in which he believed and by his example encouraged and persuaded his people to follow his lead. They were intelligent men able to discern that what is true is true and that what is false is false and people recognised that they were both perceptive and courageous. "Great men are they who see that spiritual is stronger than any material force, that thought rules the world." (Emerson) These seven understood that and applied this philosophy and for that reason have earned recognition, appreciation and gratitude.

Chapter 1

Jeremy Taylor
1613-1667

The one thing which should give Christian people a sense of proportion is the realization of the historicity of the Faith: the recognition that generations of believers have worshipped, worked and lived out their lives where we live, and that from the beginning people like us have made their contributions, just as we do, to the life of the Church. It is an adventure in imaginations to conjure up pictures of those who preceded us, and an exercise in humility when we discover how they faced up to the demands of Christ upon them. Most of them were little people who came and went making a minute impression on the events of their day and time. Occasionally men of importance appeared to give substance to the continuing acts of the apostles of Jesus Christ. They are the recognisable figures of church history. They have a fame and a value by example, for those who have the sense to learn from them and to be; influenced by what they can teach about life, and about commitment to Christ and the Church. They demonstrate the strengths and weaknesses of our common Christianity to make us proud of them often, but sometimes repelled by them. Usually they do both things to us, for even the most famous and most admirable Christians are good, bad and indifferent in turn. They demonstrate constantly the old adage that one should not put too much dependence on any man or woman. There is nothing simple about people, "nothing as queer as folks." When there is the sensible valuation of men and women and no glamourising of the more attractive among them, true likelinesses are possible. An accurate picture must show them "warts and all." Understanding of the kind means that we can have a look at someone and be impressed or distressed by what we see and not be surprised either way. Not to be commended is the modern tendency to denigrate someone who earned the respect of his contemporaries and the esteem of successive generations. Debunking has become the hobby of many biographers. We shall not be guilty of that in this profile of a churchman whose remains were laid to rest in the Cathedral Church of Dromore, Co Down, as long ago as 1667. His name is known still in that town and in Lisburn where in the Cathedral there is a memorial to him. Jeremy Taylor is the best known 17th century divine in Ireland for the reasons that his episcopate made a lasting impression on religious life and church order in Ireland; and because his writings continue to affect the thinking of scholars, and clergy and laity, on theological, liturgical and sociological matters of universal application and common concern. This Caroline divine was a remarkable man by any standards and a peculiarly saintly and learned churchman.

Early years
He was born at Cambridge, England, in 1613 where his father, Nicholas Taylor, was a barber and churchwarden. Taylor never claimed origins of greater distinction but there were those who tried to make him a kinsman of Rowland Taylor the chaplain of Archbishop Thomas Cranmer and a sharer of his fate for he, too, was burned at the stake as a heretic in the Marian persecution of Protestants. Relationship with a martyr would have been a proud distinction when open antagonism to English Papal influence was very strong, but there is no evidence for the claim. As a boy Taylor was fortunate to obtain a place in a new school founded by Stephen Perse and later a bursary to Gonville and Caius College, Cambridge, where he may have been a thirteen-year-old entrant. There are well attested cases of young boys being admitted to university in those days. He graduated BA 1630/1, and in 1633, as a Junior Fellow doing postgraduate studies he was permitted to take pupils. He was a Cambridge contemporary of John Milton, George Herbert and Henry More who were to become among the greatest figures in English literature.

Engraved by H.Adlard, from an Original Painting in the Hall of All Souls College, Oxford.

JEREMY. TAYLOR.

Bishop of Down, Connor and Dromore

London. Published by Longman & Cº and the other Proprietors.

He was influenced in his youth by the saintly Lancelot Andrewes, successively Bishop of Chichester, Ely and Winchester, who took a leading part in the Hampton Court Conference of 1604. Andrewes was the friend and confidant of King James 1 and the main influence in the formation of distinctively Anglican theology, which in reaction to the rigidity of Puritanism, was to be reasonable in outlook and Catholic in tone. In his lifetime his fame rested on his preaching. He earned the funeral eulogy that he was "a wise prelate, a great and good man, whose memory is precious and held in honour".

Taylor developed early a sense of the godly which he communicated by spoken and written word, and with a quality of selflessness which impressed all who knew him. The standards of theological thought and literary achievement were high in Taylor's time. The standards of Christian work and witness were low. These were the days of absentee incumbents and poorly paid stand-in curates and of clergy whose impoverished circumstances compelled them to be teachers and fringe medicine doctors until a convocation held at Westminster under George Abbot, Archbishop of Canterbury, in 1613 forbade them to exercise physic except in their own parishes, and for charity. And so the lines of demarcation were drawn between ministry and medicine. Taylor was ordained - the date is not certain - though Dean Comber mentions "the most famously learned Bishop Ussher (was) ordained before he was twenty-one: and the pious and eloquent Bishop, Jeremy Taylor, who entered into Orders younger than he."

Taylor became a Reader in Rhetoric and Master of Arts. He was a bright, handsome young man of engaging manner and already regarded as an able preacher. He was fortunate to come under the patronage of Archbishop William Laud, the most powerful man in the Church of England, described by one critic as a sincere man of large learning but small sense. He was a Protestant but his opinions were so near to those of Roman Catholics it was said that the Pope wanted to make him a cardinal. He was such a thorough-going Episcopalian that he had no qualms when those who condemned bishops were chastised for their audacity. Laud believed that the more ceremony there was in a church service and the more beautiful the church the greater would be the religious devotion of the congregation. The Puritans thought oppositely - that ceremony and ornament distracted the worshippers from their prayers and were therefore harmful. When Laud heard Taylor in St Paul's Cathedral for the first time he raised the objection that he was too young, at which Taylor begged his pardon and promised that if he lived he would mend it. In spite of his youth Laud must have been impressed by Taylor, the preacher and the wit, for he appointed him a Fellow of All Souls College Oxford.

In 1638 Taylor left university teaching for the incumbency of Uppingham, Rutlandshire, to which he had been appointed by the Bishop of London. There he preached on 5th November the Gunpowder Plot sermon which has the distinction of being the first of his sermons to be printed. It was hardly a masterpiece, for it was described as dull, overloaded with quotations and mere cant. He dedicated it to Laud in a fulsome form of words, typical of the time, describing himself as his Grace's "most obliged and observant chaplain, Jeremy Taylor." He was to be addicted to this kind of flattery of those to whom he felt indebted. By the influence of Laud he became a chaplain to King Charles 1. He was always a convinced and committed Royalist.

Taylor was married on 27th May 1638 to Phoebe Landisdale. Their first child, William, died and was buried in Uppingham Churchyard in 1642. At Uppingham, Taylor was regarded as a High Churchman. A critic described him in 1641 as among those who were forcing the Church of England into extremes of doctrine and practice not allowed by law. After three years at Uppingham he signed his name for the last time in the parish register. It was then he answered the call of the king to his subjects to join him in his struggle against his enemies. He did not go from the parish voluntarily, for in a note in the Cavalier newssheet, probably on information supplied by Taylor himself, it says,

> "at Uppingham, in Rutlandshire, the members have placed one Isaac Massey to teach the people for the true pastor, Dr Jeremy Taylor, for his learning and loyalty is driven thence, his house plundered, his estate seized and his family driven out of doors."

He had by then completed the manuscript of his important book, *Episcopacy Asserted*. When the king read it he conferred a Doctor of Divinity degree on Taylor. It was dedicated to Sir Christopher Hatton, and not to Laud, for Laud was a prisoner in the Tower of London and not to be further embarrassed by association with a book which pleaded the case of kings and queens and bishops together. The subject was exceedingly distasteful to a parliament determined to destroy both royalty and episcopacy. The threefold theme of the book pleaded that episcopacy had its basis as a divine institution, true to Apostolic Tradition and Catholic Practice. Taylor saw the presbyterate as a second order of ministry with its origins in the seventy disciples whom Jesus sent out to preach and teach, whereas the episcopate is linked with the apostles themselves. At this time Taylor came under the influence and patronage of the Earl of Northampton and in 1643 he was appointed by the king to a living at Overstone (near Northampton) in a Royalist area, but it seems he never took up the appointment. When Northampton was killed at the battle of Hopton, 19th March 1643, Taylor was befriended by Lady Northampton. He had published *The Liberty of Prophesying showing the Unreasonableness of Proscribing to other Men's Faith and the iniquity of persecuting Different Opinions.* It was the first plea in England for toleration. It produced a deal of controversy in an age when tolerance was regarded as intolerable. Taylor's concern then and later was for practical religion rather than speculative theology. He gave an opinion to the king, 28th August, on toleration but Charles was a man of strong and determined views and the lines were drawn so indelibly between him and parliament that the word had just about gone out of use.

Ireland

John Evelyn, the diarist, first heard Taylor preach on 15th March 1654 and they became intimate friends. This was a contributory cause in Taylor's coming to Ireland in 1658. It was through Evelyn's friendship with Lord Conway that he was offered a place in that household. It was a time of fast change in religion and politics. The Rebellion of 1641 had ended with an Act of Settlement on 12th August 1652. It had aimed at overthrowing English rule in Ireland and the recovery of the estates forfeited by the Flight of the Earls in 1607, "the extirpation of Protestantism and the establishment of Romanism." Dr J.B. Woodburn states "it is certain that the main causes of rebellion were the fear of the Catholics that their religion was to be extirpated, and the desire of the dispossessed to get back the land that had been confiscated in the Plantation of Ulster."

The Rebellion of 1641 is a dark blot on Irish history. The sufferings of the Protestants were horrifying. A 10,000 strong Scottish army was sent to quell the Rebellion and to give protection to Irish Protestants. Commanded by General Robert Munroe it arrived in April 1642. The chaplains of the army took control of the church and in September 1642 the Lords and Commons passed "An Act for the utter abolishing and taking away of all archbishops, bishops, their chancellors and commissionaires, etc." so that Presbyterianism became the established form of church government from 1646 until 1660. While no Act of the Irish Parliament had proscribed episcopacy, under the Commonwealth the Irish Parliament was swept away, and Ireland, like Scotland, was given representation in a central parliament which legislated for the whole British Isles. On 1st July 1643 the Assembly of Divines meeting at Westminster produced *The Confession of Faith, The Larger Catechism* and *The Shorter Catechism, A Directory for the Public Worship of God, A Form of Presbyterian Church Government* and *A Directory for Ordination.*

The Act of Settlement regarded Ireland as forfeited property. Residents lost their land and their lives with proof of guilt for being involved in the Rebellion. The land was made vacant and partitioned into the province of Connaught and Co. Clare where the native population was thrust and the rest of Ireland in which were settled the friends of parliament, invariably English and Scottish adventurers. The landless Irish either emigrated as soldiers, indentured to labour in the West Indies plantations, or wandered about their native land begging for bread. Jeremy Taylor came to Lisburn, Co. Antrim, in 1658 because the Rawdon and Conway families, and especially Lady Dorothy Rawdon, had conceived an implacable hatred for the Commonwealth minister, Andrew Wyke, and Lord Conway was anxious to get a Churchman. He seems to have consulted John Evelyn, the famous diarist, who at once commended Jeremy Taylor.

George Rawdon was a most consequential figure in his time. He was the victor over the rebels at Lisburn after they managed to destroy the town by fire. He was named as the saviour of Ulster in his time. He built the towns of Moira and Ballynahinch. The first Lord Moira was a descendent. Rawdon's second wife, Dorothy, was the eldest daughter of Edward, Viscount Conway. They had one son, Sir Arthur Rawdon, sometime MP for Co Down. Taylor was glad to leave England, and Cromwell was so happy to see him go that he personally signed the necessary permit. Having been deprived of his English living he had suffered poverty, homelessness and imprisonment for his religious views. The hospitality of the Conways at Portmore Lodge, near Lisburn, meant that he was provided with a refuge for himself and his family. The lodge was demolished in 1761 on the extinction of the Conway peerage. There was a small church nearby which Taylor was to replace in time with his new chapel at Ballinderry.

In Ireland Taylor found a continuation of the persecution he had known in England. He was denounced by the authorities in Dublin, for baptising a child according to the form of the Book of Common Prayer. He wrote to John Evelyn,

> "I fear my place in Ireland is likely to be short, for a Presbyterian and a madman have informed against me as a dangerous man to their religion."

It is possible that he was arrested twice and taken to Dublin. One of these imprisonments in the worst of winter weather brought him a long illness. Presbyterians in the sixteenth and seventeenth centuries seem to have been obsessed with the belief that God required them to stamp out all divergence from their system of church order and government. They were not content with conformity and submission as the Episcopalians were but insisted on outraging the conscience, on destroying self-respect and making perjury compulsory.

The Solemn League and Covenant was drawn up in 1643 as terms of cooperation between Scotland and the English Parliamentarians against the King. Its second clause is "That we shall in like manner without respect of persons endeavour the extirpation of Popery, Prelacy (that is Church Government by Archbishops, Bishops, their Chancellors and Commissaries, Deans and Chapters, Archdeacons and all other ecclesiastical Officers depending on that hierarchy), superstition, heresy, schism, profaneness and whatsoever shall be found to be contrary to sound doctrine, and the power of godliness, lest we partake in other men's sins and thereby be in danger to receive of their plagues; and that the Lord may be one and his name one in the three Kingdoms." The resolve of the Kirk was to allow no form of religion anywhere in the three Kingdoms except Presbyterianism.

Oliver Cromwell, the Lord Protector, died "in the midst of a storm" September 1658. His favourite daughter had died only a few months before. He had had control of the country for five years, this man who believed that his whole life and work were directed by God. A great soldier at times cruel and ruthless he was the most able stateman to govern England till that time. He refused the title of king which was offered to him by Parliament in l657. From 1649 to 1660 there was no King and no Church of England officially. Cromwell was succeeded by his son, Richard, nick-named "Tumble-down Dick" whose rule lasted only till May 1659. Another son, Henry, had ruled Ireland as Lord Lieutenant from 1656 to 1659.

Taylor signed the declaration, of loyalist support for the restoration of the Monarchy in London in 1660. General George Monck was the prime mover in the campaign. It was he who announced the death of Oliver Cromwell and proclaimed the succession of Richard Cromwell. Later ennobled as the Duke of Albemarle Monck foresaw the early end to Cromwell's tenure of office and prepared for the accession to the Throne of Charles 11.

From the Restoration, religious life in Ireland flowed in three distinct and clearly defined streams - Anglicanism, Presbyterianism and Romanism. Taylor dedicated his next book *Ductor Dubitantium* (the Rule of Conscience) to King Charles 11. The subject was casuistry and had four sections on Conscience, Divine Laws, Human Laws, Good and Evil.

Jeremy Taylor was consecrated bishop on l8th January 1661. A few months after his return King Charles announced his intention of restoring the Irish Church to her old position, declared that she had forfeited none of her real rights during the years of usurpation, and proceeded to fill up the vacant bishoprics, whose income had been appropriated by the Puritan party. One of the vacant bishoprics was Armagh, and to it Bramhall, the Bishop of Derry was appointed. And on 27th January 1661 two archbishops and ten bishops were consecrated in St Patrick's Cathedral, Dublin, by Bramhall and four assisting bishops. Among the bishops then consecrated was Jeremy Taylor, one of the most eloquent and saintly of Irish prelates.

Taylor was the preacher and his text was Luke 12: 42, 43, the story of the Faithful Steward and his theme 'Episcopacy'. He found the diocese of Down and Connor in a most neglected state. He wrote,

> "I perceive myself thrown into a place of torment. The ministers are implacable. They talk of resisting unto blood and stir up the people to sedition."

He also told the Duke of Ormonde, Lord Lieutenant, that he would rather be "a poor curate in village church than a bishop over such intolerable persons." The offenders were the Presbyterian ministers who had settled from Scotland since their coming in 1609. No organised body can exist without discipline. It must have rules which bind it together and these must be enforced if the organisation is to continue its existence. He argued that episcopacy is a root principle in Anglicanism. These strong convictions and the strength of the law behind him persuaded Taylor to expel from the churches of his diocese those Presbyterian ministers who had taken the places of the Church of Ireland clergy ousted from the churches by Parliament. He did not move against them until he had tried to persuade them to acknowledge and accept episcopacy. Some did, but many did not. The recognition of other ministries was not an immediate issue. On their own submissions as to church order and government the Scottish ministers had no claim on their ministries except that of occupation. Rights belonged to the bishops and the Established Church in which they were serving.

A number of early Presbyterian ministers had accepted episcopal ordination. Barkley gives a list of twenty-seven men, eight of whom were ordained by the Scottish born bishops Echlin (Down and Connor, 1613-34) and Knox (Raphoe, 1611-32). Knox had been presbyterally ordained by the presbytery of Paisley in 1581. He became Bishop of the Isles in 1605. There is also a list of ministers deposed by Echlin and Leslie (Raphoe) when the Laudian views of royalty and episcopacy- were enforced. It should have been clear from the earliest days of the Plantation that a confrontation between the bishops and the Presbyterians was inevitable. The Presbyterian historian, Professor A Buick Knox, says "The division had to come, and to romanticise about the early years of the Scottish settlement in Ulster is to be quite blind to the ultimate aims of the Presbyterians and to what a bishop who wished to be faithful to his vows would have to do." The matter was brought to a head when Sir Thomas Wentworth, later Earl of Strafford, became Lord Deputy of Ireland, for from 1633-40 he ruled the country with the single aim to destroy every force which refused to recognise the royal supremacy. His ecclesiastical reforms were carried out by Archbishop Laud and John Bramhall who had been appointed Bishop of Derry in 1634. That was the year when Wentworth forced the adoption of the English Thirty-Nine Articles of Religion on the Church of Ireland. They did not represent the views of the Irish clergy who were generally Calvinist in theology. Forced divisions seldom elicit agreeable responses. As Dr E.A. Payne points out, "The religious policy of Archbishop Laud played an important part in precipitating the Civil War."

Pastoralia

Taylor's first visitation sermon as a bishop was "The Minister's Duty in Life and Doctrine." It had two parts, "the first was an exhortation to live a holy life and preach sound doctrine; the second was on the subject of the preaching. He provided a hand-out for the clergy, *Rules and Advices to the Clergy of Down and Connor for their deportment in their Personal and Public Capacity.* It had eighty-three suggestions and many perceptive students of theology and pastoralia believe that it should have been published as *Holy Living* and *Holy Dying* had been. They felt that its value could have been similar to theirs. Taylor had neither See House nor Cathedral in his diocese. He lived with the Hills at Hillsborough House until a permanent Bishop's House could be provided for him. At 1661 Down Cathedral had been in ruins for 150 years and so in 1662, the church at Lisburn was constituted a Cathedral by Royal Charter. Taylor's early experiences in his diocese were such that it should be no surprise to find that he had hoped for a translation to Meath diocese in the wake of his predecessor, Henry Leslie, who had died in that See. He made a case for himself by pleading that the diocese of Dromore, with its dignitaries and five clergy should be added to Down and Connor under one bishop. The Bishop of Dromore was Robert Leslie, son of Henry, and Taylor hoped for his succession to Down and Connor with Dromore. But Leslie was translated to Raphoe and Henry Jones, Bishop of Clogher, was translated to Meath and Taylor became administrator of Dromore. Dromore Cathedral had been in ruins from the Rebellion of 1641. Taylor had it rebuilt in simple style. The nave was paid for out of public subscriptions and the chancel from his own pocket. The Holy Communion plate was the gift of Mrs Taylor. St Malachi's Church was built at Hillsborough in Taylor's time; to be replaced a century later by the present very fine edifice. He built the Jeremy Taylor church at Ballinderry, known as the 'Middle Church' It was restored at the beginning of this century and reconsecrated in October 1902. The Cathedral Church of Dromore is small, yet it is commodious and decent; it is not built in the manner of Cathedrals in form of a cross, nor is there any pre-venue for supporting Cathedral Service. Upon a rising ground near the church an Episcopal House was carried on by Bishop Buckworth, 1641. But the Popish Rebellion unexpectedly breaking out in the same year the House with the Town and Church, were totally destroyed, the Bishop at a few hours warning, being forced to flee for the preservation of his life to Lisburn, and from thence to England where he died in 1652. The Church lay in ruins until it was rebuilt after the Restoration by Bishop Taylor and dedicated to

Christ the Redeemer, as appears by the Altar-Plate which he gave to the Church.

Prayer

The publication of *A Directory of Public Worship* to supplant the *Book of Common Prayer* elicited a response from Taylor in 1646 when he wrote *A Discourse of Prayer Extempore*. A later 1649 edition was titled, *An Apology for Authorised and Set Forms of Liturgy.* The book was a collection of tracts dedicated to King Charles 1. On extemporary prayer "there are the questions, whether it is better to pray to God with consideration or without? Whether is the wiser man of the two, he who thinks and deliberates what to say, or he who utters his mind as fast as it comes?" He added "there is no promise in Scripture that he who prays extempore shall be heard the better."

Jeremy Taylor was living at Golden Grove, the home of Lady Northampton, when he wrote *The Great Exemplar* of which it was said "his concern was not so much with instruction as devotion, he wished to make men love God and one another more." The book was an innovation in Christian literature, for it was the first life of Jesus Christ written in English. Taylor's great devotional works, *The Rule and Exercises of Holy Living* (1650) and *The Rule and Exercises of Holy Dying* (1651) remain classics in their field. Taylor lost his wife in 1651 and Lady Northampton had died suddenly in 1650. The depth of his grief is reflected in *Holy Dying*, a more profound book than *Holy Living*. The first chapter of *Holy Dying*, may well have reached the heights of Taylor's literary achievements. He was imprisoned 1655 in the Castle of Chepstow as a Royalist. The proscriptions on Royalists were published that year. They included the advisement that to have or to be a chaplain, tutor, preacher, or to administer the sacrament, perform the marriage ceremony, use the Prayer Book or keep a school was prohibited.

From Chepstow he went to an estate in Wales, Mandinam, with Joanna Bridges, whom he had married in 1656. Because of the incidence of infant mortality the Taylors were bereaved of six sons. His two marriages produced one son, Charles, who died at 24yrs, and three daughters, Phoebe who remained a spinster, Mary who married Francis Marsh, and Joanna the wife of Edward Morrison, MP for Lisburn. Joanna's daughter married Sir Cecil Wray and earned a reputation for originating some myths about her maternal grandfather. Taylor must have been esteemed by his colleagues for on occasion he acted as their spokesman. When the Bishop of Down and Connor took his seat in the Irish House of Lords on 8th May 1661 he was described as having "the greatest reputation of any preacher in Ireland."

As the Presbyterians went about building their churches there were those who believed that Taylor should have tried harder to keep them in the Church but the attitudes of the time made that impossible. They had sixty congregations in 1661 and a hundred by 1690. The growth and early development was possible because the Presbyterian ministers suffered no molestation from Church or State.

His final days
When his son died at 24yrs in London - he was buried in St Margaret's Churchyard on 2nd August 1667. Taylor was sick with fever contracted when visiting a

parishioner. He died on 13th August 1667 at Castle Street, Lisburn. He expressed the wish to be buried at Ballinderry but as the graveyard there was not yet consecrated he was laid to rest on his death-bed wish in Dromore Cathedral. It seems that four Bishops of Dromore were interred in a vault in the Cathedral chancel - Taylor, George Rust, Essex Digby and Capell Wisemen.

The most distasteful things happen when men are greedy for office. Taylor's son-in-law, Dr Edward Marsh, Dean of Armagh, was so anxious to succeed him that he hurried off to Dublin to plead his claim to the See while his father-in-law was being waked. He was not favoured though later he became Bishop of Limerick and Archbishop of Dublin. The funeral oration was by George Rust who was to become Bishop of Dromore shortly, afterwards. Sir George Rawdon wrote from Lisburn to describe the last days of Jeremy Taylor:

> "The Bishop of Down has been very ill for three or four days, and we fear a change here; but this morning the doctors gave more hope of his recovery than yesterday, when the Lord Primate took leave of him. I insinuated to his Grace yesterday (in case the Bishop should die) for worthiness of the Deans of Connor and Armagh to succeed, for it will be two Bishoprics hereafter. I do not know whether at the distance you are you can have a voice in the choice of the next Bishop. His Lordship has made a will, and has not in all £2000 to dispose of, of which £600 is for his lady and two daughters."

Rawdon wrote again on 14th August.

"The Bishop of Down died about three yesterday afternoon and has left a sad family. He was in such a fever for several days that he could not make a will, and had I not reminded him to do so, he would have died intestate. We are much mistaken in his estate, for he has only left £1500 on Lord Donegal's hands, and £600 which your Lordship has to pay. Unless we advance £100 of this I do not know how the funeral charges will be met for there is no money in the house. There are two doctors, one from Dublin, to be paid, and his lady cannot pay them-without borrowing. Dean Marsh has gone to Dublin, having, I think, some hope of being his father's successor in the See of Down and Connor, and I have used all endeavours with the Primate and Chancellor, and mentioned your favours in order to get the Bishopric of Dromore for the Dean of Connor. Please write to the Lord Lieutenant in his favour and use your influence to stop any letter that may be sent to Court for any other person (to have the See). I am writing to Lord Orrory to use his influence with the Lord Chancellor in the same direction. We are saddened by the Bishop's death and the distress of his family. I have been very importunate with the Primate and Lord Chancellor that the half rent due next Michaelmas may be reserved for her and for the two daughters unpreferred. His Lordship desired to be buried in the church he built at Dromore, or at Ballinderry, if it should be consecrated before his death, but it is not so. They are putting his body sear cloth, which will not be buried till the Dean of Armagh returns.

There was another letter on 31st August:

    "The very night the Bishop died the orchard was broken into and the fruit all stolen. Some loose timber, which was very dry and unseasoned was also taken. The funeral is to be on Tuesday, and the body was sent in my old coach to Dromore church. I have now got a letter from the Primate which makes me think all my requests will be granted - the Dean of Armagh for Down and Connor, the Dean of Connor for Dromore, and that the widow shall have the half year rents. Your Lordship's help must be in England with the King or the Archbishop of Canterbury to prevent anyone else but the Dean of Connor being made Bishop of Dromore."

Memorial

There was no monument to Jeremy Taylor in the United Diocese until Bishop Richard Mant had a fine mural tablet in his memory placed in Lisburn Cathedral. The inscription written by Mant reads:

Not to perpetuate the memory of one, whose words will be his most enduring memorial, but that there will not be wanting a public testimony to his memory in the diocese which derives honour from his superintendence. This tablet is inscribed with the name of Jeremy Taylor, D.D., who on the restoration in M.DC.LX. of the British Church and Monarchy, in the fall of which he had partaken, Having been promoted to the bishopric of Down and Connor, and having presided for seven years in that See, as also over the adjoining diocese of Dromore, which was soon as after instructed to his care, "On account of his virtue, Wisdom, and industry;" Died at Lisburn; Aug. 13 M.DC.LXVII

The Middle Church Ballinderry

in the 55th year of his age; leaving behind him a renown. Second to that of none of his illustrious sons whom the Anglican Church, Rich in worthies hath brought forth: As a Bishop distinguished for Munificence and Vigilance truly episcopal. As a theologian for piety the most ardent learning the most extensive and eloquence inimitable; In his writings a persuasive guide. . .', to earnestness- of devotion. uprightness of practice, and Christian forbearance and toleration; a powerful assertor of Episcopal government, and liturgical worship, and an able exposer of the errors of the Romish Church; In his manners a pattern of his own rules Of holy living and holy dying, and a follower of the GREAT EXEMPLAR of sanctity as portrayed by him in Person of OUR LORD and SAVIOUR JESUS CHRIST. Reader, though it fall not to thy lot to attain the intellectual excellence of this Master in Israel, thou mayest rival him in that which was the highest scope of his ambition, an honest conscience and a Christian life.

Dr Rust in his funeral oration paid high compliment to the work and worth of Taylor. After references to his scholarship, his eloquence as a preacher and his humour, he said,

> "he had nothing in him of pride and humour, but was courteous and affable, and easy of access, and I would lend a ready ear to the complaints, yea to the impertinencies of the meanest persons and to all other virtues added a large and diffusive charity; and whoever compares his plentiful incomes with the inconsiderable estate

he left at his death, will be easily convinced that charity was steward for a great proportion of his revenue. But the hungry that he fed, and the naked that he clothed, and the distressed that he supplied, and the fatherless that he provided for; the poor children that he put to apprentice, and brought up at school, and maintained at the university; will sound a trumpet so that charity which he dispersed with his right hand, but would not suffer his left hand to have any knowledge of it."

Hensley Henson observed:

"Jeremy Taylor is not the only example our ecclesiastical history affords of a brilliant, versatile, learned bishop prematurely broken down by the relentless stupidity of fanaticism. He is the most contradictory and many-sided figure in the long gallery of great Anglicans. One of the earliest advocates of theological liberty, he was vehemently denounced by his contemporaries as an ecclesiastical persecutor, the chief of our anti-Roman controversialists; he was also the most sympathetic with ideas and practices which are commonly associated with the Roman Church. Alone of his contemporaries he remains living influence on religious thought and action. It would be impossible to discover any weightier evidence on his transcendent merit.

Short Episcopate
Jeremy Taylor made such an impression as a bishop that it is easy to overlook the fact that his episcopate lasted only seven years. But he lived to see the better ordered Church of Ireland, growing in influence and with much of its property, which had been confiscated by Cromwell, restored to it. His influence remains and entirely for good in his prayers and devotional works. His contribution to liturgy, was considerable. He was credited with the authorship of the Form of the Consecration of a Church in the Irish Prayer Book. His *Collection of Offices*, 1658 was intended for the use of Anglicans in the times when the Book of Common Prayer was proscribed. It was sufficiently unlike the Prayer Book to be technically legal, but close enough to the genius of that book to preserve the essentials of Anglican worship. It contains daily offices, communion, baptism and burial services and prayers for various occasions. Harry Boone Porter writing on the subject says:

> "There is a consistency between the private and the public prayers, and between the prayers and the discursive discussions. The same themes and the same doctrines appear again and again, phrased now one way and now another, made vivid by a kaleidoscopic variety of metaphors and verbal pictures, fortified by scriptural references, illuminated by decrees of councils and the sentences of divines and sayings of philosophers, and an endless selection of stories and strange incidents from every age of history. It is this ability to state his ideas with such a variety of expression, and to relate them to the fabric of

human life with such a richness and penetration
of insight, which is the magic of Jeremy Taylor."
Jeremy Taylor remains a champion of Anglicanism and
of the Church of Ireland which he served selflessly, for
his defence is seen constantly as relevant when there are
questionings of its legitimacy. Taylor writes:

> "We have the Word of God, the Faith of the
> Apostles, the Creeds of the Primitive Church, the
> articles of the first four General Councils, a holy
> liturgy, excellent prayers, perfect Sacraments, faith
> and repentance, the Ten Commandments and the
> sermons of Christ, and all the precepts and
> counsels of the Gospel. 'We teach the necessity of
> good works… we communicate often. We are
> enjoined to receive the Holy Sacrament thrice
> every year at least. Our priests absolve the
> penitent. Our bishops ordain priests, and confirm
> baptized persons, and bless their people and
> intercede for them. And what could here be
> wanting to salvation?"

His strong biblicism which remains a characteristic of
Irish Anglicanism was always evident in what he wrote
and preached. He judged that "the Scriptures do not
contain in them all things necessary for salvation, is the
fountain of many grave and capital errors." In a judgment
on Taylor's episcopate Harry Boone Porter points out: "It
was Taylor's destiny to live and die in an age of intense
religious conflicts, when those very convictions often
seemed to divide those whom they should have united."

Studies

An attempt was made in the years 1968 -1985 to study the worth and work of Jeremy Taylor by annual lectures in Dromore Cathedral. The early ones were well suited to that purpose but later lectures bore little resemblance to what was originally intended so that they became unattached from Taylor studies and petered out. There was the problem of numbers attending so that early on the Cathedral Chapter, who wanted a sizable audience for its guest lecturers, combined the lecture with a cathedral event like the installation of dignitaries. The arrangement ensured good attendances but of people often with little or no interest in the lectures. It would have been wiser to keep the lectures of such academic and practical value that they would have attracted their own audiences, size being of no consequence. Better to have a small group of interested people than a large number who were present only for the sake of appearances. The experience of those years meant that an experiment of the kind was not attempted until 1992 when Dr H.R.McAdoo gave a Jeremy Taylor Memorial Lecture on 14th May in Dromore Cathedral. It was titled "The Practising Christian: Jeremy Taylor on Believing and Behaving." The only Jeremy Taylor lecture to be published as a booklet by a Dean and Chapter of the cathedral it has a foreword by the Bishop Dr Gordon McMullan. In it he said,

> "In his Jeremy Taylor *Selected Works* Dr Thomas K Carroll notes Dr McAdoo's scholarship wherein he describes him as the former Archbishop of Dublin and primate of Ireland, who has brought to light, for the first time the theological modernity of Taylor. Dr McAdoo's

task is to show that Taylor's chief concern is with the practical, with the realities of believing and behaving in a complicated world."

He quotes him:

"Christianity is all for practice and so much time as is spent in quarrels about it, is a diminution to its interest. Men inquire so much what it is, that they have but little time left to be Christians. The way to judge of religion is by doing our duty: and the theology is rather a Divine life than a Divine knowledge."

"The Practising Christian" is McAdoo's application of Jeremy Taylor's thinking, teaching and practice to this day and time. He emphasises these in references to his writings which were always devotional and practical. The question is asked, could Taylor's view of the practising Christian be a realistic view for our times and answers in the affirmative. Taylor's evaluation of man remains relevant, for he is the same in his need to recognise realities which though affected by change stay constant in spite of change. There is the Christian imperative, "All true manliness grows around a core of divineness." (Charles H Parkhurst)

Chapter 2

George Walker
1649-1690

N one of those involved in one of the most momentous, horrible and magnificent, happenings in Irish history - the Siege of Londonderry - had a more important role to play than the Rev George Walker. For he was at once the most highly honoured and esteemed among the commanders of the garrison - feted by the king, and cities and colleges - but also the most reviled, because he had an enemy unfair, unbalanced and unscrupulous and who was believed by a few historians and writers who accepted the charges against him and sometimes added to them without justification or evidence. Walker was a third generation clergyman. His grandfather Gervase Walker was Rector of Cappagh and Badoney in the Diocese of Derry from 1626 and was buried in Derry Cathedral in 1642. His father, George Walker was in 1617 a Scholar of Trinity College Dublin and succeeded his father as Rector of Cappagh and Badoney, but fled to England in the Rebellion of 1641. He returned to Ireland at the restoration of the monarchy in 1660. He was married probably in 1642 to Ursula the eldest daughter of Sir John Stanhope, Melwood, Yorkshire. She died in 1654 according to a tablet in Wighill Church, near to Kirk Deighton, and there her daughter Margaret was baptised in 1650. In 1662 George Walker was Rector of Donaghmore and Errigale Keerogue, Chancellor of the Diocese of Armagh and Rector of Kilmore by 1664. He died in 1677 and was buried in Kilmore Church, Armagh.

Birth

George Walker of Derry was probably born in England about 1646 during his father's exile there. He was educated at Trinity College Dublin, having matriculated on 29th April 1662. He married Isabella Barclay. That information is on the Walker monument in Castlecaufield Church, which was erected by his widow and shows the arms of the Walker and Barclay families intertwined. They had five sons and three daughters. Three of his sons were with Walker in Londonderry 1689 and four of them served with him in the Battle of the Boyne 1690. The pressures of King James on Protestants, in his determination to promote Roman Catholicism produced reactions which culminated in armed resistance. Walker was among those clergymen who recognised that the future of Protestantism in Ireland was bleak if the King had his way. There were three attitudes among Protestants - those who were frightened, intimidated and submitted: the despairing who fled to England: and those who stood together against the pressures of Romanism. Early in 1689 Walker raised an army in Dungannon. In those days it was not unusual for clergymen to be "militarily involved" as leaders of their people. John Leslie, Bishop of Raphoe and Clogher, had taken part in armed campaigns against the rebels of 1641 and the Cromwellians. His prayer on the eve of battle was said to be:

> "Almighty God, if we be sinners they are not saints, though Thou vouchsafest not to be with us, be not against us but stand neuter this day and let the arms of flesh decide it."

The Protestant fears had been expressed in preparations to prevent a massacre like that of 1641. They began to take steps for their defence and enrol armed volunteers. In March the leaders and their forces met in Hillsborough but Tyrconnell's Army dispatched from Dublin compelled them to retreat to North Antrim and Derry. Strong bodies of Protestants assembled in Enniskillen and Sligo. King William, not only approved of Protestant resistance, he was willing to issue commissions to any officers who took up arms against the Jacobites. While Tyrconnel, King James' top man in Ireland, threatened severest punishment on all who opposed him, and pardons for those who submitted to him.

James in Ireland

War broke out in March 1689. James had landed in Ireland from France where he had been living, in exile the guest of Louis XIV, on 12th March. The die was now cast. All hope of an arrangement had disappeared and the only resource left was to decide the dispute by force of arms. Walker claimed that as clergymen are allowed to be capable of the privileges of mankind and of all the creatures in the world, they may all defend themselves and there may be such necessity upon them that it is their duty to do it. He maintained that the man who did not was guilty of *felo de se*. He explained his position. The lives of thousands beside his own were at stake. His religion that was dearer to him than they all, and the English and Scotch equally dear to him, were next door to an utter extirpation out of that Kingdom not to speak of the dangers of others. How can any imagine that there should be an obligation upon any man that can exempt him or excuse his unconcernedness in such a case.

During the latter part of March and beginning of April 1689 the Protestant forces held Coleraine and the line of the Bann. Driven from there they fell back on Londonderry and the rivers Finn and Mourne. On 11th April George Walker rode in haste to Derry to inform the Governor Lundy that the enemy was approaching, but the governor professed to believe that it was only a false alarm. Walker returned to Lifford an angry man. That night he and Colonel Crofton defended Clady Fort against the advance of the Irish forces and at the Long Causey without any assistance from Lundy. Later when he and his men went to add their strength to the Derry garrison they found the gates of the city closed against them and they were compelled to spend the night outside the walls. Next day when Colonel Adam Murray and his troops arrived at the gates they too were refused admittance but the captain of the guard disobeyed Lundy's orders and they entered the city. Two days later King James and his army were camped in sight of Derry.

The Governors

On 10th April Lundy having been removed from his office for dereliction of duty as evidenced by the unpreparedness of the people of the city to defend themselves, Major Henry Baker and the Rev George Walker were appointed joint-governors. They faced an apparently impossible task, the defence of the city, which had been described as indefensible by an experienced military man. A poem in the rhyming chronicles "Londerias" by Joseph Aicken, a doctor, who rendered great service during the Siege, describes what happened.

> "Then all with one consent
> Agreed upon this form of Government:
> Baker and Walker, Governors they chose
> And formed eight regiments to oppose the foes.
> The Governors all matters soon dispose.
> Baker and Walker mutually consent
> To settle quarters and to regulate
> The stores over which Harvey a merchant's set.
> The town into four quarters they divide
> And place two regiments in every side.
> The Council and the Governors decree
> That all the officers should together be.
> Upon such grievances we changed the powers
> And add a Council to the Governors.
> This raised great anger to the Governors

Had they sent aid the trenches had been ours.
The Governors divide the joyful store
And equal portions give to rich and poor."

Baker was to be the governor responsible for defence while Walker's main task was to be in charge of stores and the welfare of the civilian population. He had the added duty of encouraging soldiers and citizens alike to face up courageously and defiantly to whatever lay ahead of them. His vigorous, unpolished, but effective rhetoric was to prove to be a morale booster to the besieged. And he made contact with those outside the walls who were sympathetic to their cause. It was his name which appears first on all official documents and papers.

A method of soldiering was agreed by common consent. Eight colonels were nominated and the soldiers chose their captains. In turn each captain decided on which colonel he would serve under. Evidence was provided that Walker was respected as a soldier - he had been nominated as one of the colonels - when fifteen captains chose him while twenty-five chose Baker and seventeen Mitchelburne. *A Journal of the Siege of Londonderry, in a letter from an officer in the town* dated 15th May has this description of Walker's activities:

> "Mr Walker caused a parley to be beat and desired a cessation of arms that day (12th) to better solemnise the Sabbath which was agreed. That day Colonel Walker preached, taking as his text, 'The Sword of Gideon and of the Lord.' He exhorted the soldiers vehemently to courage and resolution, telling them that on their valour relied the safety of the three Kingdoms and bid them to be ready for some great action."

In an account of a rally on 16th May there is this from the same officer:

> "On our approach we received three discharges from their trenches, but Colonel Walker gave order that no man should fire a gun till we came within half pistol shot of the trenches, when doubling our ranks we poured on them three volleys of shot."

News of the Siege of Derry was eagerly awaited in Great Britain. Information was conveyed by newsletters and pamphlets and Macauley tells how the popular excitement was reflected in parliament. Whatever disagreements there were among members on other matters they were agreed in their admiration of the defenders of Derry. Honest John Birch expressed their feelings:

> "This is no time to be counting cost. Are those brave fellows in Londonderry to be deserted? If we lose them will not all the world cry shame on us? A Boom across the river: Why have we not cut the Boom in pieces? Are our brethren to perish almost in sight of England, within a few hours voyage off our shores?"

Walker featured so frequently in these cross-channel papers that his participation in the Siege was well known and it produced general admiration even in the palace. Lady Shatsworth in a letter to the Earl of Rutland dated 3rd May 1689 said: "Our King the other day drank the victorious Mr Walker's health and said he had rather see him than any man in the world." The Siege lasted 105 days. Out of 7300 fighting men engaged in it 4300 survived though 1000 of them were mentally and physically unfit for any kind of military service. It was such a horrific happening that it compares in suffering with some of the worst cases of similar kind. "The people died so fast that there was no room to bury them, even the backsides and gardens were filled up with graves, and some thrown in the cellars."

Walker Honoured

When Derry was relieved the Council sent Walker to London with an address to King William and Queen Mary dated 29th July 1689 and carrying the signatures of 145 of the principal survivors. On the journey he received several honours - the freedom of the city of Glasgow on 13th August and of Edinburgh on 14 August when the parchment was written in letters of gold. At Chester on 22nd August Mr H Prescott, the Registrar of the Chancellor of the diocese, writing of Walker's visit described how the General, the Mayor and all the officers welcomed and entertained him in the dining hall of the town. He said: "When he walks abroad the people accompany him: gather in knots about him and follow him in crowds. Admiring him as if he had dropped from heaven they gaze on him with greedy and excited ears."
Walker was met at Barnet by Sir Robert Cotton and taken by coach to London where he was received with enthusiasm by large crowds. No less liberal were they in their applauses and commendations: extolling his fame in verses and panegyrics; publishing his effigies in printed cuts, tossing his name between printers and hawkers and making it the subjects of news-letters and gazettes; while every man according to his family proportioned a reward

to his unrequited merits. It seemed as if London extended him a Roman triumph and the whole kingdom to be actors or spectators of the cavalcade. At last he arrived, the King received him graciously and conferred on him a mark of his favour and esteem. The Lords of the Council and several of the nobility caressed him with abundance of kindness and respect. The prime citizens treated him with all the demonstrations of joy and gratitude; and the vulgar even stifled him with gazing, crowding and acclamation. The letter from a fulsome admirer said: "Sir, it was my good fortune on Wednesday last to meet Mr George Walker, the Famous and Fortunate Governor of Londonderry."

The Irish Society gave a banquet in his honour and he was received in audience by the King who ordered that his portrait be painted by Sir Godfrey Kneller. The House of Commons voted him a gift of £5000 on 18th November. He petitioned Parliament for relief for the widows and orphans of Derry and for the clergymen who had helped considerably in the Siege. He was received in the House on 19th November to be told by the Speaker that he had the thanks of parliament and that they were petitioning the King to give £10,000 for the relief of the people of Derry. The Speaker went on to say:

> "They will likewise take notice of the extraordinary service you have done to their Majesties and to England and Ireland, in defence of Londonderry, and especially in that you undertook it when those to whose care it was committed did shamefully, if not perfidiously, desert their places; and have thought fit to show a particular esteem of your merit, and give you the thanks of the House, and they would have you

give the thanks of this House to all those that were in that service."

Walker also appealed to the Irish Society for financial relief for the impoverished city and succeeded so well that it applied to the Lord Mayor, Aldermen and Common Council to persuade the twelve chief London companies to give £100 each. The money having been obtained it was distributed among the sufferers of the Siege. On 8th October 1689 he had been awarded a Doctor of Divinity degree by Cambridge University and on 11th February 1690 he received a DD degree from Oxford University. The citation read: "Reverend George Walker, that strenuous and unconquered defender of the City of Derry, and by that deed we trust, the preserver and deliverer of all Ireland."

Archbishop Tillotson writing to Lady Russell on 7th September 1689 said:

> "The King beside his great bounty to Mr Walker (£5000) whose modesty equals his merit, hath made him Bishop of Londonderry, one of the best Bishoprics in Ireland. It is incredible how much everybody is pleased with what his Majesty hath done in this matter, and it is no small joy to me that God directs him so wisely."

Hopkins

Bishop Ezekiel Hopkins had fled from Derry to London and became Rector of St Mary, Aldermanbury. He died on 19th June 1690 and thereafter the See was declared vacant. It would appear then that what William had done was to offer the bishopric to Walker when the vacancy occurred. Because Hopkins has been maligned by some historians of the Siege it is necessary to say something about him. He came to Ireland as the chaplain of the Viceroy, the Earl of Radnor, and married his daughter. He was appointed Bishop of Raphoe in 1671 and was translated to Derry in 1681. A man of substance he presented Derry Cathedral with an organ and Holy Communion plate. A writer, his collected works were published in 1701. They appeared again in four volumes in 1809 and in two volumes in 1841. A Calvinist his articles were published by the Religious Tract Society in *The Writings of the Doctrinal Puritans of the 17th century.* He was described by his contemporaries as "modest, hospitable and charitable: a great preacher and no inconsiderable poet." His books were purchased for the Derry Diocesan Library by a successor Bishop King. Hopkins believed in "passive obedience" a common attitude among the clergy of his time, but he had to change his views when he realised that what King James intended was the destruction of his church. He was unhappy, as were most of the important people of the city, when on 7th December 1688 the apprentices closed the gates.

The reason for the action was that by the beginning of December the Protestants of Ulster anxious about Viceroy Tyrconnel's policy for Ireland, were fearful of a massacre like that of 1641. The famous Comber letter telling them that this massacre would take place on 9th December put them into a panic. The letter was found in a Comber, Co Down, street on about the 1st December, the date it carried, and addressed to Lord Mount-Alexander. It was written in an illiterate hand, real or bogus, and warned of the massacre of Protestants on 9th

December 1688 by Roman Catholics who would be rewarded for their murders. The letter was accepted as genuine and the writer thanked for giving such timely warning to people in grave danger. Copies were sent to Dublin and Londonderry where it arrived on 7th December. Whoever wrote the letter and whatever his intentions - the warning had no basis in fact - it started in train events which resulted in the Siege of Londonderry and the loss of Ireland to King James. When the men in Derry received the letter they also heard of the approach to the city of Lord Antrim's regiment being sent on Tyrconnel's orders to replace one which had been ordered from the city to leave it without a resident regiment. The civic authorities there and the rest of the graver citizens were under great disorder and consternation and knew not what to resolve upon. While they hesitated Lord Antrim's regiment of Irish and Highland Scots came within sixty yards of Derry. It was then that a number of youths, the famous Thirteen Apprentice Boys, took control and shut the gates in the face of the government troops. By their audacious act they made possible the defence of Derry in 1689. W S Kerr says "It shows how the unrestrainable instinct of the crowd can sometimes be wiser than the cautious deliberations of officials and seniors."

While some of the prominent citizens of the city were sympathetic to the action of the apprentices they were all fearful of the consequences, for the Closing of the Gates was an act of rebellion against the only sovereign of the realm, King James, and the city was totally unprepared to repel the royal forces. The gates were closed at about noon and that evening a meeting of the important citizens was held in the market place. They were anxious to point out what could be the dangerous results of defying the government of the kingdom. Hopkins was one of the speakers and he counselled caution. "Londerias" put his sentiments into verse.

> While they debated thus another came,
> With weeping eyes and thus accosted them:
> Dear friends a war upon yourselves you'll bring
> Talbot's deputed by a lawful King.
> They that resist his power do God withstand,
> You'll draw a potent army to this land
> Who will these goodly buildings soon deface
> Ravish your wives and daughters fore your face,
> And all your wealth and substance soon devour
> Submit yourselves unto the present power.

W.S. Kerr makes the comment:

> "It is easy for us to ridicule the advice of the Bishop and to rejoice that more vigorous counsels prevailed. If we put ourselves however in the position of the responsible citizens of Derry that day we can easily understand why they could not countenance what had been done."

The feeling that Hopkins expressed was strong among the people for Derry had only about 300 men fit to bear arms. There was little food and guns and ammunition were scarce. The city was saved in 1688 only because Tyrconnel had not enough men to send against it. And the show of defiance by the apprentices had its effect, for when terms were made with the viceroy conditions favourable for Derry were obtained. King James' troops were allowed into the city, but it was Lord Mountjoy's Protestant regiment and not the Roman Catholic one of Lord Antrim. Two weeks after the closing of the gates the articles were agreed on with Mountjoy. In them the citizens declared that the action of 7th December was for self-preservation and they disclaimed all tincture of rebellion, perverseness, and wilful disobedience to the King's authority and the established laws of the land. The danger remained for no one doubted that Tyrconnel's policy of Protestant extirpation had not changed, and preparations were put in hand to ensure a greater readiness for the next and inevitable emergency. Provisions were obtained on a large scale and guns and ammunition procured from several sources. In the months between the closing of the gates and the Siege, the Ulster Protestants had organised the defences of Derry and in April men from the northern counties, willing to fight for the Protestant cause were gathering there. As important as all this King William now on the British throne, issued commissions to the Ulster officers and sent Captain James Hamilton with large supplies of money and ammunition. But earlier the citizens of Derry had disassociated themselves from the performance of the apprentices and expressed loyalty to King James. The mayor, John Campsie and Alderman Norman wrote to Lord Mountjoy on 9th December and said:

> "The last post carried up to his Excellency the news of what our rabble had done in the town, how they had shut the gates against some of the Earl of Antrim's regiment which we then blamed them for but could not restrain them the rabble in their heat found means to get into the magazine and thence took some arms and ammunition, but

we have caused it to be locked up and guard set thereon."

They went on to explain the people's terror because of the bad reputation of Antrim's soldiers and the prospect of another awful massacre and said:

"We cannot but think it a most wonderful providence of God to stir up the mobile for our safety and preservation of the peace of the Kingdom against such bloody attempts as these Northern people had formed against us which we doubt not but his Excellency will look upon as a great and very acceptable service to his Majesty to whom we resolve always to bear true faith and allegiance against all disturbers of his Government whatsoever."

There was dependence on Mountjoy to make their peace with Tyrconnel. On 10th December Mr David Cairns, the leading citizen, was sent to London with a declaration of similar kind to be presented to the Irish Society. The signatures included Mr H Phillips, the Governor, by appointment of the citizens, Mayor Campsie and Aldermen Norman, Tomkins and Cocken. It ended: "that Mr Cairns be assisted to secure us from the common danger and that we may peaceably live, obeying his Majesty, doing injury to no man nor wishing it to any." Added to this was *A Declaration of the Inhabitants of Derry* explaining that it was "the younger and some the meaner sort of inhabitants" who shut the gates "obstinately refusing obedience to us."

"We have firmly and sincerely determined to persevere in our loyalty to our sovereign lord the

King without the least umbrage of mutiny or seditious opposition to his royal commands. God save the King."

It was obvious then that Bishop Hopkins when he counselled caution was only echoing the sentiments of the people generally, for all of them acknowledged James' sovereignty. Professor Witherow explains:

"As yet they had not declared for the Prince of Orange - they were not averse from the troops of King James provided only that they were Protestants; and they were most unwilling that their recent action should be interpreted so as to bear the appearance of disloyalty and rebellion."

The attempt to pillory Hopkins for being faithless to Protestantism or King William is reprehensible. But then the criticisms of the bishop came much later. The Rev Joseph Boyse, the Presbyterian controversialist of the time pays this compliment to Hopkins:

"I think he would do the greatest wrong to the reputation of that ornament of his profession the Reverend Bishop of Derry who should brand him as one of Tyrconnel's agents, or a well wisher to the Irish and Papal interests, because he advised the inhabitants of the city to open the gates after the first shutting of them; chiefly I doubt not out of a real dread of these dismal consequences he apprehended would ensure on so dreadful an undertaking."

Gordon

Those who contrasted Hopkins' attitude with that of the Rev James Gordon, who advised the closing of the gates and of Alex Irwin, who is said to have interrupted the Bishop's speech were being grossly unfair to Hopkins. Actions speak louder than words for neither of these men were within Derry's walls in April 1689. The comparison Hopkins and Gordon, the Presbyterian minister of Glendermott, is an unfortunate one for Gordon. Hopkins was a man of exemplary character and creditable attainments. Gordon was a notorious reprobate. J.M. Bulloch, LL.D., FSA., the distinguished literary man and antiquarian, who made a study of Gordon titled his pamphlet, *The Reverend James Gordon, Sensualist, Spy, Strategist and Soothsayer.* He was all these things and stood condemned by the Presbyterian Church in Scotland where he had been ordained. There appeared to be no depths to which he would not sink. He sought in 1682 the help of the Bishop of Edinburgh to obtain Anglican Orders after telling him that in London falling unluckily acquainted with some nonconformist preachers, was induced by them to join into their society and being by them invited to Ireland hath for these two years past preached among them near Derry. The Bishop acquainted the Duke of Ormonde, with the "seen the error of his ways hath of his own accord come hither to discover to Lord Deputy information of Ireland, the that Gordon having my Lord Chancellor of Scotland and to me several important matters which he is ready to impart to your Lordship." Gordon received the commendation of the Lord Chancellor and the Bishop as an informer who could be useful to Ormonde. Bishop Hopkins to whom the matter was referred, wrote to Ormonde of how he had been visited by Gordon who told him of a plot between the Presbyterians of Ireland and of Scotland; that collections were being taken in their congregations for the redemption of Christian slaves but that the money was being used to buy arms for rebellion against the Government, and that next spring they expect a ship with arms at Portaferry in the County of Down or somewhere thereabout. Hopkins appears to have taken pity on Gordon and offered to give him money to go to Dublin if the Viceroy wanted to see him. The Archbishop of Armagh wrote Hopkins that the Duke proposed using Gordon as an informer but asked the Bishop to enquire into his reputation. Hopkins found many people willing to testify against Gordon as a rogue and a rascal and wrote the Primate that "Gordon intends to make himself by this new trade." On 9th January 1683 Bishop Hopkins wrote that he considered Gordon to be a mere juggler with one design to be admitted into the ministry of the Church of Ireland. Because he was "infamous among his own party" and "unfit to be owned of any" he advised against employing him even as an informer for "to handle such a tool would only smut the hand that toucheth it."

He was never used by the authorities. However Gordon died in the odour of sanctity as Minister of Cardross Church in Dumbartonshire where he enjoyed some respect as a prophet and soothsayer. He claimed that it was he who persuaded Kirk to attempt the Breaking of the Boom. Kerr judges that "notwithstanding the attitude of the Rev James Gordon at the Shutting of the Gates, we can still maintain that every man of responsible position and trusted judgement in Derry was opposed to raising the standard of rebellion there in December 1688." When it came to a choice, James or William, Hopkins chose William and was named as a traitor by James' parliament in Dublin. He had his income seized by King James and supported himself as a London vicar until his death in l690. Kerr describes the attacks made by the Presbyterian historians Killen, Latimer, Hamilton, Moody, Hopkins and Walker, and shows them to be unfair and discredited by their misinterpretations of the events in which the men were involved. The intention of these historians was to show that Presbyterian participation in the Siege was much greater than Walker appeared to allow. But they did him and his fellow Episcopalians an injustice for they had never denied the size and quality of the Presbyterian involvement.

Walker Dishonoured

What Walker wrote in *True Account of the Siege of Londonderry* licensed 18th September 1689, incensed the Rev John Mackenzie, Minister of Cookstown Presbyterian Church, who charged him with dishonourable conduct in his dealings with Governor Lundy before the Siege; during it as the steward of stores - he refused to recognise him as Governor and even hinted at immoral behaviour. Walker admitted that he had made mistakes in a publication that had been too hurriedly produced but pleaded no ill intention. In his *Vindication of the True Account* an answer to charges made in Mackenzie's *A Narrative of the Siege of Londonderry, or the late Memorable Transactions of that city. Faithfully represented to rectify the Mistakes and supply the Omissions of Mr Walker's account,* London 1690, he pleads with those that have used him with such severity that the very errors of the printer were charged upon him; the importunity and forwardness to get the book out of his hands much quicker than he intended so that it neither so perfect nor so correct as it should have been. When he found the mistakes he excused himself by thinking that most people would be kind enough to make allowances to be expected of one who was not used to such a task. Mackenzie presents Walker as an impostor who falsely claimed to be Governor; a traitor to the garrison; guilty of criminal acts and of immoral practices. There is no denying that Walker was Governor. Gervais Squire, Mayor of Derry, put that fact beyond doubt when he said:

> "I administered the said oath (of fidelity) to the said Dr Walker and Colonel Baker as Governors of the said city (the said Dr Walker having the precedence) as well as to the members of the said Council, all of which I am ready to depose upon oath if required."

As to Walker's honesty there is the testimony of Edward Curling:

> "And I do further declare that I was made storekeeper of the provisions at the beginning of the Siege, and continued so to the end, and did from time to time deliver out provisions upon the said Dr Walker's order as Governor, in which station he continued in great esteem among us, until the said city was relieved by Major-General Kirk, and I never knew his order disputed during the whole time of the Siege; and I do look upon the said Pamphlet as to what relates to the said Dr to be not only false but scandalous and malicious."

No case was ever made against Walker for indecency or unethical conduct.

As to Walker's influence in Derry there is the testimony of King James who kept a careful record of his experiences. He tells that when he reached Omagh in 1689 he received a letter from the Duke of Berwick assuring him that he had only to show himself at Derry for it to surrender. But finding that the city acted differently he wrote:

> "What made the town in such different minds was the arrival of one Walker, a minister, who had put himself at the head of the rebels at Dungannon and then abandoning of it at the King's approach retired to Londonderry; before his arrival Lundy the Governor thought the place untenable and resolved to leave the town and men at liberty to make such conditions as they thought best, but this fierce minister of the Gospel being of the true Cromwellian and Cameronian stamp inspired them with bolder resolutions and the Col. Cunningham and Richard who had brought from England two regiments, ammunition, provisions, etc., were forced to return without getting that relief into the town. Nevertheless they resolved to bid defiance to the King and their true allegiance choosing this minister and one Baker to be colleagues in the government of the place and gave the first check to his Majesty's progress."

W.S.Kerr contends that had Mackenzie "confined himself to a temperate criticism of the defects of Walker's writings he would have been listened to. But his virulence and the palpable absurdity of most of his charges have left Walker's renown unharmed."

Even so Kerr describes Mackenzie's narrative as a valuable one. It is much better written than Walker's for he was a much more accomplished writer. Regrettably bitterness was allowed to cloud his judgement and it caused him to write half-truths and untruths about his opponent. He waged a lone vendetta against Walker and was discredited by contemporaries who disagreed with many of his claims, charges and conclusions. That did not prevent Presbyterian historians of a century and centuries later, from quoting him as the most creditable source on the Siege. It was a question of denominationalism and rivalry.

On the Walker and Mackenzie controversy W.S. Kerr makes the relevant comment:

> "It is a pitiable thing that men who came through such sufferings together, linked by common interests, should afterwards be engaged in sectarian wangling; and that one denomination should strive to claim the glory for its own members and discredit that of others."

In the late seventeenth century relations between the churches were poor. Each had suffered at the hands of the other; and experienced the effects of supremacy the one over the other. The Church of Ireland oppressed Dissenters; the Presbyterians abhorred toleration and compelled consent to the Solemn League and Covenant which said:

> "That we shall in like manner without respect of persons endeavour the extirpation of Popery, Prelacy (that is church government by Archbishops, Bishops, their Chancellors and Commissaries, Deans and Chapters,

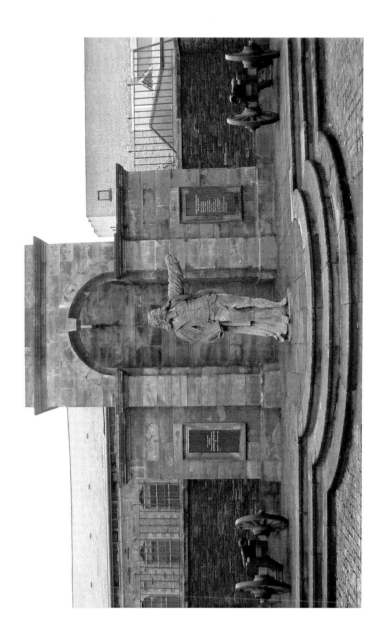

Archdeacons and all other ecclesiastical officers depending on that hierarchy) superstition, heresy, schism, profaneness and whatsoever shall be found to be contrary to sound doctrine and the power of godliness lest we partake in other men's sins and thereby be in danger to receive their plagues; and that the Lord may be one and His name one in three kingdoms."

George Walker's father had shared the sufferings of his church when he had been forced to live in England at the suppression of the Church of Ireland. The Belfast Presbytery in its 1649 declaration denounced the Commonwealth authorities for trying to establish by law an universal toleration of all religions which is an avowed overturning of unity in religion and so repugnant to the Word of God and the first two articles in the Covenant. The Rev Patrick Adair, minister of Belfast, protested against the wickedness of Cromwell in carrying on "a course of lawless liberty of conscience." And the system denounced excluded Episcopalians and Romanists from toleration. After the Siege, Walker returned to his parish in Co Tyrone. He was one of those who met King William at Carrickfergus on 14th June 1690. Walter Harris writes:

"His Majesty was attended by the nobility, gentry and clergy of those parts and presented with an address of congratulation by Dr Walker in the name of the Episcopal clergy, introduced by the Dukes Schomberg and Ormonde; and with another from the several Presbyterian ministers both of which he received very graciously."

Walker was with the King at the Battle of the Boyne as chaplain of the Royal Army. There he showed reckless courage when he went to the assistance of the Duke of Schomberg who was rallying the Huguenots in the thick of the battle. Story, who was at the battle says:

> "Dr Walker going as some say to look after the Duke was shot a little beyond the river and stripped immediately, for the Scottish Irish that followed our Camp were got through already and took off most of the plunder."

Gideon Bonnivert, who was also at the Boyne, recorded in his journal: "That day we lost Duke Schomberg and Dr Walker, Governor of Londonderry. They were killed in forcing the passage." The old story that when William heard of Walker's death he said, "Fool that he was, what had he to do there?" has no basis in contemporary literature. It appeared only when Sir John Dalrymple "who drew on his imagination to make history picturesque" wrote *Memoirs of Great Britain and Ireland* a century later.

William's opinion of Walker is best expressed in a medal he had struck to memoralise the victory of the Boyne. It shows the King on horseback and James running from him. Then, as Harris describes it "a little lower down Duke Schomberg and Dr Walker lie dead on the opposite bank of the river."

Walker was buried at the Boyne but in 1702 his widow had his remains re-interred in Castlecaufield Church. The body was identified by William Blacker of Carrickblacker who served at the Boyne with a company of volunteers which he had raised himself. Mrs Walker placed a monument to him in the church. The translation of the Latin is:

> "P.M.S. Near this Reader are deposited the remains of the Rev George Walker, Doctor of Sacred Theology, formerly Rector of this parish. He, whose vigilance and valour Londonderry in the year 1689 was rescued from the enemies of William and the faith, fell mortally wounded on the banks of the Boyne for the same cause against the same enemy in the year 1690, to whose remains and memory his inconsolable widow Isabella Walker has erected this monument in the year 1703. But his fame will be more durable than rock, nor shall future ages less than the present admire a soldier so pious and a minister so intrepid."

A monument was erected to George Walker in Derry in 1826 - a pillar of Portland stone, 81 feet high, placed on the Royal Bastion and surmounted by a statue of the Governor in the clerical dress of the seventeenth century. The right hand held the Bible, the left pointed down the river Foyle towards the site of the boom, supposedly calling attention to the approach of the Mountjoy and her companions, The inscription on the pillar read:

> "This monument was erected to perpetuate the memory of the Reverend George Walker who, aided by the garrison and brave defenders of the city, most gallantly defended it through the protracted siege from the 7th December 1688 O.S. to the 12th August following, against an arbitrary and bigoted monarch, heading an army of 20,000 men, many of whom were foreign

mercenaries. And by such valiant conduct, in numerous sorties, and by patiently enduring extreme privations and sufferings, successfully resisted the besiegers and preserved for their posterity the blessing of civil and religious liberty."

The monument was blown up by the IRA in 1973. A replacement was erected in 1992.

Effects

The Siege of Derry and the Battle of the Boyne had national and international implications. Not only the liberties of Ireland and Great Britain were in jeopardy, the scheme of King Louis XIV of France for domination as aborted on the banks of the Foyle and the Boyne. Professor G.M.Trevelyan explains:

"The racial war for the possession of the island involved the fate of England and of Europe. Before Britain could send her armies to fight France on the Continent she had first to secure her shores... all who rejoice that the Protestant communities of Europe maintained their freedom against Louis and destroyed the prestige of his system on the fields of Blenheim and Ramilles, must read with thankfulness the story of that initial passage of the Boyne which first gave stability to the Revolution settlement."

R.H.Murray evaluated the position:

"For little as he realised it the French King received a fatal blow from the citizens of a petty town in the North of Ireland... The men of Derry stood between Louis and ascendancy in Europe. Their conduct during the Siege proved to the world that they were willing to sacrifice themselves to the uttermost for the cause they held dear. Like their King they felt there was one way never to be defeated and that was to die in the last ditch."

In the darkest days of the Siege, George Walker was to record: "They will not entertain the least thought of surrendering, and it would cost a man's life to speak of it, it was so much abhorred." Sir G.O.Trevelyan summed up the situation of Derry when he said:

> "Still as in Londonderry of old the real strength of a besieged place consists not in the scientific construction of its defences, nor in the multitude of the garrison, nor in abundant stores of provisions and ordnance, but in the spirit which is prepared to dare all and endure all, sooner than allow the assailants to set foot within the wall."

The Rev George Walker was the respected leader of a people who earned and retained the respect of all who regard as sacrosanct the right of individuals, communities and nations to fight for principle and survival.

Chapter 3

Jonathan Swift
1667-1745

M any clergymen have made an impression on people and events in their day. A few of them are famous. Some of them were highly respected for bringing credit to Christ and the Church and benefit to those among whom they lived and were committed to serve. Others are remembered for less worthy reasons. No clergyman in Ireland in his lifetime, made an impression greater than that of Jonathan Swift who was ordained on 28th October 1694 in Christ Church Cathedral, Dublin, by William Moreton, Bishop of Kildare and Dean of the cathedral. After three years as a deacon he was provided with the tiny prebend of Kilroot in the Diocese of Connor. He ministered there, unhappily, for some eighteen months, for he hated the place only a little less than the Presbyterians who formed the bulk of the community and his congregation. Before he left Kilroot he proposed marraige to Miss Jane Waring, sister of a college friend and daughter of a tanner in Waring Street; Belfast, but the proposal was refused because the lady, he called her Varina, was confused, bullied and astonished by it. No wonder for he asked her,

> "Are you in a condition to manage domestic affairs with an income of less, perhaps, than £100 a year? Will you be ready to engage in those methods I shall direct for the improvement of your mind without being miserable when we are neither visiting nor being visited? If so, I shall be blest to have you, without regarding whether your person be beautiful or your fortune large".

Years after when he had made a way for himself she was refused when she sought him for he said: "She that will not when she may, When she will I'll say here nay." He was cruel for he told her that when he wanted her she could have had him, but he was not to be fingerwagged at her pleasure. He reminded her that she had £100 a year, enough to take her out of such a sink as Belfast, or if she chose to stay in the sink, she had her mother and her Belfast society, of whom she appeared to be fond, but for neither of which he had any fancy.

What Swift wrote, and what has been written about him, has caused him to remain a man of consequence and influence in Irish life and literature. Among the major works on him are *The Pen and the Sword: Jonathan Swift and the Power of the Press* by Michael Foot (1984); *Jonathan Swift, a hypocrite reversed - a critical biography* by David Nokes (1985); and *Jonathan Swift and the Art of Raillery* by Charles Peake (1986). Swift's thinking on religion and politics continues to have relevance, because tensions and controversies remain and political unease between Britain and Ireland continues.

Birth

Jonathan Swift was born on 10th November 1667 at Hoey's Court, not a stones throw from St Patrick's Cathedral, Dublin, of English parents. And into a tragic situation for his father Steward of the King's Inns, Dublin, had died eight months before. His mother Abigail was already struggling to rear a brother and sister, Thomas and Jane. The infant was carried off by his nurse to her family home at Whitehaven in England where he remained for about three years. A precocious child, he was able to read before he returned to Ireland and the care of his mother. At six he was a boarder at Kilkenny College where the fees were paid by a reluctant uncle, Godwin Swift, lawyer and speculator, of whom Swift was to say, "He gave me the education of a dog." A fellow pupil was William Congreve who was to become famous as writer and poet. At fifteen Swift entered Trinity College, Dublin, where he was neither happy nor industrious. He graduated through the kindness of his examiners. Among his contemporaries at TCD were Thomas Wilson, who was Bishop of Sodor and Man for sixty years; Edward Chandler, Bishop of Lichfield and later of Durham, an appointment it was said he had obtained with a bribe of £9000; and Peter Browne, Bishop of Cork and Ross, and famous for his discourses against drinking in memory of the dead and in particular of King William Ill.

Refugee

When King William pursued King James 11 to Ireland in 1688 Swift was one of the refugees who fled to England. He lived with his mother there. Through her friendship with Dorothy Osborne, the wife of Sir William Temple, he became a secretary at his home, Moor Park, Surrey. Temple was the English diplomat who negotiated the Triple Alliance of 1688 between England, Holland and Sweden. It was he who arranged the marriage of Mary, niece of the reigning King Charles 11 and daughter of his brother and successor, James II, with William, Prince of Orange. They were to become joint sovereigns as King William III and Queen Mary 11. It was at Moor Park that Swift met William and formed what he hoped would be a profitable relationship for him. There, too, he met Hesther Johnston, a ward of Temple's and his pupil from when she was six years of age. Stella as he called her was to become his companion for most of her life. Swift left Moor Park in 1694 with the intention of working in the office of the Master of the Rolls in Dublin but he was disappointed when someone was preferred to him.

Ordination

It was then he sought Holy Orders, was ordained and later appointed to Kilroot, Co Antrim. His short stay there was followed by another at Moor Park, Surrey,

1696-1699. He left there when Sir William died. That was when he discovered the foolishness of putting one's trust in princes, for King William who had promised him an appointment either at Westminster Abbey or Canterbury Cathedral, failed him. He went to Ireland with the Lord Chief Justice, the Earl of Berkeley, and with a promise of a government appointment but again he was disappointed when someone else got the job. He might have become Dean of Derry had he had £1000 the amount of money needed to buy the deanery. The Rev John Bolton, Rector of Laracor, Co Meath, provided the cash and when he went to Derry Swift succeeded him at Laracor. The gift of the Prebend of Dunlavin gave him an income of £244 a year. Those were the days when a curate could be "passing rich" on £40 per annum. The Laramor congregation was tiny with three prominent families. Swift described them in a letter to Laurence Sterne dated 17th April 1710, "Mr Percival is Ditching, Mrs Percival in her Kitchen, Mr Wesley Stitching, Sir Arthur Langford Riching." The Wesleys were good friends to Swift but Percival's son Robert, the MP for Trim deprived him of half his tithes and received a rollicking from him. Langford was so partial to Presbyterians that he brought on himself the wrath of Swift. Swift spent his holidays at Virginia Water, Co Cavan, with Dr Thomas Sheridan his old schoolmaster where he wrote much of *Gulliver's Travels.* The giant of the book was based on a local character, Big Doughty, a very large man. He held the incumbency of Laracor, in plurality until his death and it was there he was to find his retreat from the pressures of life in Dublin. In 1709 hearing that Bishop Downes of Cork was on his death bed, Swift wrote Charles Montagu, first Earl of Halifax, asking to be considered for the See when it became vacant.

Dean

Jonathan Swift was installed as Dean of St Patrick's Cathedral, Dublin, on 13th June 1713. Swift was thrilled with his appointment in what he described as "absolutely the greatest cathedral in the Kingdom." With his deanship went another office that of administrator of the liberty of St Patrick's. He was to refer to himself as Lord Mayor of 120 houses. When Swift took office the cathedral was in poor shape. He took control at once and immediately met with opposition from members of the Chapter and gentlemen of the choir. He was soon in dispute too with William King, Archbishop of Dublin. They were politically in disagreement for King was a Tory and Swift a Whig. They had two things in common, though, a strong objection to the policy of the government to fill Irish bishoprics with English clergy; and a commitment to promoting the spiritual and temporal welfare of the Church of Ireland. It was fortunate that these two able men declared a truce and developed a kind of partnership of mutual advantage. Swift's appointment as dean produced a skit from Jonathan Smedley, Dean of Killala. "This place he got by wit and rhyme, And many ways most odd, And might a bishop be in time, Did he believe in God." This view of Swift was echoed by the Earl of Nottingham who described him as "a certain divine who is hardly suspected of being a Christian" but is "in a fair way to become a bishop." Dr Samuel Johnston was more accurate in his assessment of Swift when he explained:

"The suspicions of his irreligion proceeded in a great measure from his dread of hypocrisy; instead of wishing to seem better, he delighted in seeming worse than he was."

Lord Bolingbroke spoke of him as "a hypocrite inverted." David Nokes urges his readers to recognise the essential honesty and humanity of Swift that made him prefer to seem a monster rather than a hypocrite. Swift had a total distaste for sentimentalism, a disregard for religious enthusiasm which showed in an outward facade of piety and a cynical view of human nature. He was unwilling to advertise the fact that he had a religion and yet his religion and his churchmanship were the most important things in his life. A.R.E Winnett said:

"He was before all else a Christian and a churchman, and the church's wellbeing as he understood it, was a central not merely a peripheral concern of his life."

The many sidedness of Jonathan Swift has been recognised - pamphleteer, political lobbyist and poet - but above all, and regulating everything was the fact that he was primarily a churchman.

Cathedral

Swift with a remarkable persistence and patience won over the chapter, for by strength of will and certainty of purpose he convinced them that his way was best. Because Swift recognised the value of music and singing in the worship of the church, while not being musical himself, he determined to have a choir which would be a credit to his cathedral. He was determined that its members would be the best singers available. The choristers were selected only on ability and suitability. Influence would not be allowed to take the place of competence. When Lady Carteret, the wife of the Viceroy, tried to obtain a place in the choir for a friend he told her he would use his influence to get him a deanery or a bishopric since efficiency was not essential in these offices, but he had to refuse her request, for choirmen were severely tested every day. A choirman who had absented himself from church for several days reappeared to sing the anthem, "whither shall I go from thy spirit or whither shall I flee from thy presence?" (Psalm 130:7) The dean growled in an audible whisper, "To jail, you dog, to jail." After having trouble with the choir, the members being subdued, he punished them by demanding that "the monies forfeited by the vicars choral for their absence and neglect of their duty in the cathedral be disposed off in wainscoting for the Vicar's Hall." He ordered the Sub-Dean and Chapter to "preserve the dignity of my station and honour of my chapter (by punishing) such vicars as shall ever appear as songsters, fiddlers, pipers, trumpeters, drummers, drum-majors, or in any sonal quality, according to the flagitious aggravations of their respective disobedience, rebellion, perfidy and ingratitude." At the end of the dean's ministry the famous St Patrick's Cathedral choir sang to George F Handel's accompaniment when "The Messiah" was first sung in Dublin in 1742. Swift explained his attitude to music in church in a letter to Lady Carteret:

> "For my own part, I would rather say my prayers without it. But so long as it is thought by the skilful to contribute to the dignity of public worship, by the blessing of God it shall never be

disgraced by me; nor, I hope, by any of my successors."

Tory

Swift was a Whig who became a Tory. The Irish Whigs were described as the "Cromwellian Vultures" while the Tories, apart from a small number of country gentlemen, among them the Duke of Ormonde, were "the enslaved masses of the Catholic Irish." In Ireland to be a Tory was to be a Jacobite was to take your stand with the victims of the penal laws under which they suffered. The change of political allegiance put his career in jeopardy and brought threats on his life. He was booed by a Whig mob as he walked the streets of Dublin. He involved himself in Jacobite plots and was warned by a friend, Erasmus that if he had not hidden his papers in some secret place or put them in the care of a trusted friend they would be likely to fall into the hands of enemies and he would be punished. Swift's own safety never appeared to bother him for he never lacked courage and he was a stubborn man. He claimed independence for Ireland which he regarded as a distinct kingdom, with its own rights and responsibilities. He asserted,

> "The English parliament had no more right to make laws for Ireland than the Irish parliament had to make laws for England… the laws of God, of nature, of nations, and for your own country, you are and ought to be as free people as your brethren in England."

He posed the question, "Am I a free man in England and do I become a slave in six hours by crossing the channel?" The Anglo-Irish were not all of a mind with

Swift. Grattan, Burke, Tone, graduates too of Trinity College, Dublin had different political attitudes and aspirations. J.C.Beckett points out that:

> "Swift exiled in Dublin had become the champion of Irish independence; Burke successfully settled in England, became the champion of English control over Ireland."

Burke had a different perception out of his experience and saw the importance to the British Empire of a happy and peaceful Ireland. He stated his view in a letter of 1796. "Ireland cannot be separated one moment from England without losing every sense of her present prosperity and even every hope of the future." Wolfe Tone saw the influence of England as of disadvantage to Ireland. Grattan would have widened the view of Swift by having Roman Catholics fully involved in the whole life of the country." J C Beckett explains:

> "Swift and Grattan represent the mainstream of Anglo-Irish thinking in the eighteenth century; Burke with his view of Ireland as a dependent but vitally important member of the world-wide empire looked to the future. But where are we to find room for Wolfe Tone who rejected alike the Protestant exclusiveness of Swift, the parliamentary conservatism of Grattan and the imperialism of Burke, and who devoted his life to the establishment of an independent and democratic Irish republic?"

Tone had the support of many Irish people, some of them Ulstermen and Presbyterians. They were to be the leaders and soldiers of the 1798 United Irishmen's Rebellion and for which some of them were exiled and others executed. Tone who founded the movement in 1791 unsuccessfully sought French aid for a revolt against British rule. Captured he was sentenced to death but committed suicide in 1798.   The great period of the Anglo-Irish was the period 1690-1810. It began in the wake of the Glorious Revolution and ended with the parliamentary union between Great Britain and Ireland. It opened with "confident expectation and ended in bloodshed disillusionment and a sense of betrayal."

Writer

Jonathan Swift always wrote for a purpose to make society recognise what was wrong with it and to persuade it to change itself. He used his pen to rescue a friend, to savage an opponent, to serve a cause. At the beginning he established himself as a most formidable pamphleteer and an indomitable force for change. He used satire with its chief instruments irony, sarcasm, invective, wit and humour. He may have been the creator of taut modern English: as an original thinker he copied no one. His *Drapier's Letters* published anonymously in 1704 were written in the guise of a drapier anxious to stop a fraudulent conspiracy before Ireland's trade was ruined by it. What began with, anger and agitation on Swift's part snowballed to become a major problem which involved, everybody from the Viceroy to the poorest citizen.

Bruce Arnold explains the need for the Dean's campaign:
    "William Wood had bought from the Duchess of
    Kendal a patent for £10,000 giving the right to
    introduce into Ireland a base metal coinage… the

Irish Parliament voted against the measure and Swift undertook the writing of four letters… warning the people of the great danger to the economy of a worthless coinage which would be legal tender (exchange) for Irish gold and silver. The letters had enormous effect in rousing everyone against the proposed measure, after considerable trouble, including the threat of prison for the author on whose head the Viceroy had placed a price of £500, and the actual imprisonment of the printer, the measure was abandoned, and Wood was compensated by the English Parliament for the loss of the patent. Swift received no payment for his part in the salvation of his country."

In the first of his *Drapier's Letters* Swift was typically paternalistic. He said,

"It is a great fault among you, that when a person with no other intention than to do you good, you will not be at pains to heed his advice. It is your folly, that you have no common or general interest in your view, not even the wisest among you, neither do you know or inquire or care, who are your friends, or who are your enemies."

A poet assessed Swift's success by his Letters:

The Dean did, by his pen, defeat
An infamous destructive cheat;
Taught fools their interest how to know,
And gave them arms to ward the blow.
Envy has owned it was his doing,

To save that hapless land from ruin;
While they, who at the steerage stood,
And reap'd the profit, sought his blood.

Dublin

Swift's pastoral commitments and community involvements made him fight the battles of the poor, the inarticulate and the unprotected. Bruce Arnold says:

> "It is easy to imagine Swift, in wig and clerical waistcoat, the benevolent despot, tramping the streets of the city, with one of his servants walking behind him, and playing havoc with his satirical tongue among all the elegant fashions and blind foibles of the Georgian capital… But such a view would be a misunderstanding both of the man and his Dublin. Satire is bred from a heart that feels too much the weight of human injustice and human folly, and each word or phrase is balanced with great care before being released on a highly antagonistic public; the great satirist is highly sensitive, easily moved to violent expression of his emotions, generous and fair in his dealings with people, and above all things honest… Swift was such a person. All he needed to spur him to action was injustice; and he found it in Dublin."

The Dublin of Swift's time was the victim of many economic abuses. They came from a corrupt English court and a not less corrupt Castle and Parliament in Ireland. Swift made such an impression on Dublin that he was known everywhere as "The Dean." What the Dean said made news. Lord Carteret, who had offered a reward of £500 to whoever would name the author of Drapier's Letters, in a postscript to a letter dated 24th March 1736 said: "When people ask me how I governed Ireland I say that I pleased Dr Swift."

Writings

Swift's pamphlets made demands for improvement in the economy and a better standard of living for people. They were "persuasive and full of telling strokes." His *A Tale of a Tub* was a tremendous satire on almost every established institution and custom. Clearly the work of an angry young man - Dr Johnston described it as "that wild book" - was always Swift in his aims and attitudes. Years after its publication, he exclaimed, "Good God, what a genius I had when I wrote that book." Papists and Dissenters were the main targets. Michael Foot describes it "the whole was a tour-de-force in which the author upheld the ideals of political moderation with ribald extravagances and launched his crusade for the one true Church of Christ in the language of blasphemy." Swift claimed that it was written for the universal improvement of mankind. He believed in the goodness of God but failed to see corresponding goodness in man. He was repelled by the low standards of the society in which he lived and for this reason he tried to shock the world into repentance, a turning to God and godly living. *A Tale of a Tub* tells the story of the adventures of Peter, Jack and Martin, representing the Pope, Calvin and Luther: Roman Catholics, Dissenters and the Church of England. The intolerance of the book is patent, but then religious toleration was nearly unknown at the beginning of the eighteenth century. Swift was convinced that the Church of England had a recognisable body of revealed truth. It was 'The Church'. He was strenuously opposed to both Roman Catholicism and Protestant Dissent. He lumped them contemptuously with Deism, Atheism, Socinianism, Quakerism, Muggletoniansim, Fanaticism and Brownism. He had to flee from Dublin in the short Papist ascendency under King James 11 in 1689 and he feared the growth of the Dissenters from his unhappy days at Kilroot and the deprivation and imprisonment of his grandfather, Thomas Swift, the Royalist vicar of Goodrich, by the Presbyterians in the Civil War.

Writing of the contributions of some great men to England at 1709 G.M.Trevelyn said,

"A nation of five and a half million that has Wren for its architect, Newton for its scientist, Locke for its philosopher, Bentley for its scholar, Pope for its satirist, Addison for its essayist, Bolingbroke for its orator, Swift for its pamphleteer and Marlborough to win its battles; had the recipe for the genius."

Gulliver's Travels was seen as holding a mirror up to humanity by which Swift urges man to see himself as he is, petty, gross, bestial, fantastic and contradictory. He wrote *The Conduct of the Allies* described as the most deadly pamphlet in the English language. When he opposed Marlborough "their paths crossed to provoke one of the most exciting crises in English history. The pen and the sword fought a duel, and the pen proved the stronger of the two." When Marlborough fell - he rose again - Swift said of him,

"This Lord who was beyond comparison the greatest subject in Christendom."

Social Worker

Swift was committed to the alleviation of the distresses of the "Liberty of the Dean of St Patrick's." The Liberties were semi-independent city districts with their own rulers and peculiar privileges. Because of its independence the cathedral liberty attracted to it debtors, rogues and vagabonds, some of them very violent and Swift coped with them. He advised local tradesmen on how to cope with their businesses by encouraging them to manufacture only quality goods so that customers would continue trading with them. His aims were often thwarted by poor workmanship, inefficient management and the scramble for quick profits. He supported home industries and coined the phrase, "Burn everything English except their coal." The people idolised and feared him and believed everything he said. Once a crowd gathered to see an eclipse of the sun, when they were told that the Dean had had it postponed they dispensed at once. Swift was both generous and mean. He was sparing in his own personal needs to be more able to give to the poor. He gave one third of his income to charity. Dr Patrick Delaney, his colleague and biographer, described him as "a walking parson always striding the streets to see for himself the conditions of those who sought his charity."

Living conditions in Ireland were very bad for very many people. Bishop Berkeley, the philosopher, asked in 1736, "Whether there be upon earth Christian or civilised people as beggarly wretched and destitute as the common Irish?" Swift provided indentured apprenticeships for young people by providing the bond money. He opened a bank with the first £500 of free money he possessed, lending small sums free of interest if paid back in the first year. The scheme operated for several years to put many small traders on their feet.

Stella

Esther Johnston was Swift's most intimate. She remains a figure of controversy. The relationship they had is still questioned. That he depended on her is not questioned for she was available to ease his hours of pain, to laugh depressions, to encourage him in his plans. Swift suffered from labyrinthine vertigo, a disease of the inner ear, which produced giddiness, deafness and sickness, and he dreaded insanity for his uncle Godwin had died in a mad house. Wyse Jackson, sometime Bishop of Limerick, claims that Swift and Stella married secretly in 1716. He said the ceremony was performed by the Bishop of Clogher, "though they lived separately." Other writers claim that he never married because he feared its responsibilities. A reason given for their not marrying was that he was the natural brother of Sir William Temple and she the natural daughter. Swift gave no credence to this suggestion; on the contrary when he presented a chalice to Goodrich Church it was in memory of his grandfather, Thomas Swift. Stella tried to snare him into marriage by making him jealous. She became engaged to the Rev Billy Tisdall who sought Swift's permission to marry her. He was refused as a husband on the ground that his income was not sufficient to support a wife. When Tisdall inherited enough money to overcome that objection and again sought Swift's approval on his suite he was refused again. Angrily he accused Swift of jealousy and charged him with duplicity for he was himself in love with the lady.

Swift's response came in a letter to Tisdall in which he said,

> "First, I think I have said to you before, that if my fortune and honour served me to think of that estate (matrimony) I should certainly among all the persons on earth make your choice, because I never saw that person whose conversation I entirely valued but hers: this was the utmost I ever gave way to."

The romance between Stella and Tisdall ended and he went his way unregretted, for she said he bored her to distraction with church politics. When Stella died Swift paid her the compliment, "She was the truest, most virtuous and valuable friend that I, or perhaps any other person, was blessed with."

Swift also attracted the amorous attentions of the highly emotional Esther Vanhomrigh, a Dublin girl whom he met in London and called Vanessa. He enjoyed her company and at her home in Celbridge where he found an occasional retreat. When their friendship ended she took to drink and became a lonely, tragic figure. On her death bed she refused the ministrations of a clergyman called Price to cause someone to say, "No Price, no prayers."

The Man
Swift belonged to the group of talented Irishmen as different as Yeats, Joyce, Parnell and Wilde. They were

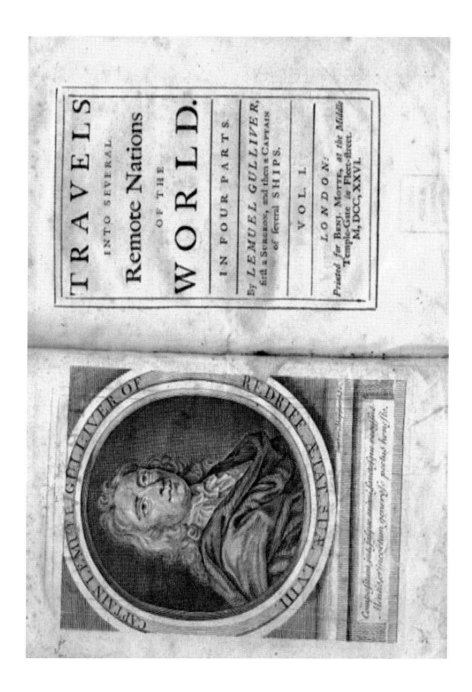

controversial characters and each of them had his own kind of genius, and all of them had tragic, destructive experiences. The arguments about Swift came from what he wrote and what was said or written about him by contemporaries and biographers. Denis Johnston says:

> "This acrimony aroused by Swift's private affairs does suggest that on the pavement of St Patrick's Cathedral there lurks, not only the bones of a master of savage indignation but also an unquiet demon of controversy that manages to entrap anybody who pauses there to ask what all the shouting is about."

Swift's greatest benefaction was St Patrick's Hospital, Dublin. The gift elicited the comment: "He gave what little wealth he had, To build a house for fools and mad; And showed by one satiric touch, No nation wanted it so much." He died on 19th October 1745 aged 78. He had spent the last five years of his life "failing in his memory and understanding, and of such unsound mind and memory that he was incapable of transacting any business or managing, conducting or taking care of his estate or person." For two days he lay in state in the Deanery Hall and Dublin paid its homage to a man respected and loved.

On 22 October at midnight, a few friends being present, he was laid to rest in the south side of the nave of his cathedral. George Faulkner, his printer and publisher, in an obituary in the "Dublin Journal" said:

> "Last Saturday at three o'clock in the afternoon died that great and eminent patriot, the Rev Dr Jonathan Swift... his Genius, Works, Learning and Charity, are so universally admired that for a

News Writer to attempt his character would be the highest presumption.. as the printer hereof is proud to acknowledge his infinite obligations to the Prodigy of Wit, he can only lament, that he is by no means equal to so bold an undertaking."

The inscription on the tombstone reads:
"Here lies the body of Dean Jonathan Swift, Of this Cathedral Church, Where savage indignation, Cannot lacerate his heart anymore, Traveller, go, And imitate if you can His strenuous vindication of Man's liberty."

There were other contemporary opinions of Jonathan Swift. Alexander Pope described him as:
"a dignified clergyman, but one who by his own confession, has composed more libels than sermons. If it be true, what I have heard often affirmed by innocent people 'That too much wit is dangerous to salvation' this unfortunate gentleman must certainly be damned to all eternity."

Joseph Addison, his good friend, acclaimed Swift as "the most agreeable of companions, the truest of friends and the greatest genius of the age."

Vocation
Swift could have had an easy life as a dignitary of the established and privileged church; and as an author of innocent fiction. Instead he used his position to fight injustice the pen to compel change of attitude among

those who had power and to encourage the common people to demand their rights. His satire was especially suited to waken people to the realities of life, for it mocked what some regarded as sacred. He had his place among the great Anglo-Irish authors like Berkeley, Burke, Goldsmith and Brinsley Sheridan. They made up a quintet of genius hardly to be matched and not surpassed among the great writers of the period. J C Beckett says: "There is no exaggeration in Yeat's proud claim for the Protestants of Ireland have created most of the modern literature of this country." Swift's literary output relatively small in quantity, places him among the great writers of English prose in any age. As a churchman Swift had a high view of episcopacy but a low view of Irish bishops. Good and saintly bishops were the exception, for many of them were Englishmen, political appointees selected for their willingness to support English policy in Ireland. Swift, angry that his ideal of Apostolic Succession had been debased described Satan as the bishop to whom many of the Irish bench were suffragans. He even suggested that some new Irish bishops had been murdered by highwaymen on Hounslow Heath on their way to Dublin and the robbers having stolen their robes and patents took their identities and used the Irish Sees. He contended that the way bishops were appointed in England killed ambition in the Irish clergy who were often discouraged from excelling in learning when obscure English clergy without academic qualifications received preferment. Swift's great ambition had been to be a bishop because of the influence he could have wielded on public affairs. He remains an example to Irish clergymen in the causes he espoused and the unselfishness he displayed in his aims and aspirations.

Swift on Preaching

There is so much in the writings of Jonathan Swift to interest and inform us that we have areas in them for subject pick and choose. Understandably my concentration is on his views and attitudes to preaching and the preacher. When allowance is made for the personal eccentricities of this remarkable clergyman there remains a repository of solid teaching on a subject that remains relevant. The church continues to emphasise the value of preaching as the main medium of communication to believers and unbelievers alike. The attempts to replace the sermon by visual representations using ancient or modern techniques have supplemented but not supplanted preaching. The growth of evangelicalism with its concentration on the Ministry of the Word could bring back an emphasis on preaching of such high standard that the churches will be renewed and enlarged. Where there is church growth - and there is this other side of the picture of Christianity - there appears to be an enthusiasm for preaching. In days when preaching was not highly valued Jonathan Swift took the craft seriously. His sermons show a style plain, direct and economical in his use of words. His method was to set out concisely what a Christian should believe and how he should behave. He saw belief and practice as the twin essentials of the Christian life. His *Letter to a Young Gentleman, Lately Entered into Holy Orders* was described as one of the most instructive treatises on the art of preaching ever written. It embodied Swift's own practice. John Wesley said, "One of the best tracts which that great man, Dean Swift, ever wrote was his sermon upon the Trinity."

Swift did not always keep his sermons. Once he gave thirty-five of them to a colleague saying, "Here is a bundle of my old sermons. You may have them if you please, they may be of use to you, they were never of any to me." The remark was hardly meant to be taken seriously.

A few quotes from his sermons show something of their quality. He concluded one,

> "God has sent us into the world to obey his commands, by doing as much good as our abilities will reach, and as little evil as our many infirmities will permit. Some He has trusted with only one talent, some with five, and some with ten. No man is without his talent, and he that is faithful or negligent in a little; shall be rewarded or punished, as well as he that hath been so in a great deal."

His sermon "On the Poor Man's' Contentment" was addressed to the "honest, industrious, artificer, the meanest sort of tradesman and the labouring man." After encouraging them to persevere in honest toil he enumerated the benefits the poor possess –

> "Health, sound sleep, freedom from hatred and the goading of ambition; while the rich live under many disadvantages - business, fear, guilt, design, anguish and vexation are continually buzzing about the curtains of the rich and the powerful, and will hardly suffer them to close their eyes unless when they are dosed with the fumes of alcohol."

In his sermon on the "Martyrdom of King Charles I" he described "those wicked Puritans" and their efforts to destroy the Established Church; and their attempts from the reign of Queen Elizabeth to remove from the clergy, surplices and ecclesiastical vestments; and from the occasional offices the ring in Holy Matrimony and the sign of the cross in Holy Baptism. He found it hard to accept that Dissenters should be called Christians "neither will the bare name of Protestants set them right, for surely Christ requires more from us than a bare profession of hating Popery, which a Turk or an Atheist may do as well as a Protestant."

Another sermon "Brotherly Love" is a savage attack on both Roman Catholics and Dissenters. He opened with:

"This nation of ours hath for a hundred years past been infested by two enemies, the Papists and the Fanatics; who each in their turns, filled it with blood and slaughter, and, for a time, destroyed both the church and the government."

After going on to describe their "inroads and insolence" he concludes,

"In order to restore brotherly love, let me earnestly exhort you to stand firm in your religion hitherto established among us without varying in the least, either to Popery on one side or to Fanaticism on the other; and in a particular manner beware of that word, moderation, and believe it, that your neighbour is not immediately a villain, a Papist and a traitor, because the fanatics and their adherents will not allow him to be a moderate man."

Standards

The Dean determined to improve the standard of preaching in his cathedral. He took out paper and pencil when a preacher entered the pulpit and carefully noted every wrong pronunciation or expression that fell from him. Whether too hard, or scholastic (and of consequence not sufficiently intelligible to a vulgar hearer) or such as he deemed in any degree improper, indecent, slovenly or mean; and those, he never failed to admonish the preacher of as soon as he came into the Chapter House.

He had no patience with the purely emotional type of preaching of the kind known among the Dissenters. He called it "handkerchief wetting" and said, "A plain convincing reason may possibly operate upon the mind both of a learned and ignorant hearer as long as they live, and will edify a thousand times more than in the art of wetting the handkerchiefs of a whole congregation, if you were sure to attain it." Sir Walter Scott said of Swift's preaching,

> "he had none of that thunder that appals, or that resistless and winning softness which melts the heart of an audience. He can never have enjoyed the triumph of uniting hundreds in one ardent sentiment of love, of terror, or of emotion."

In Swift's day the evangelistic sermon was practically unheard in the Established Church. He wrote a skit in the form of a letter on "superior preaching", as from a village schoolmaster to a country clergyman, who had a fondness for big words "in a style as near as he could to your own." It is a plea for sermons that could be understood in country parishes:

"We do, from the nadir of our rusticity, almantarise to the very zenith of your unparalleled sphere of activity, in beseeching your exuberant genius, to nutriate our rational appetites with intelligible theology, suited to our plebian apprehensions, and to recondite your acromaticall locutions. for more scholastic asculators."

What he appears to be saying is we ask you as ordinary country folk to teach us theology out of your superior knowledge, simply, and in language suitable to our understanding; and not with words used only by scholars. Swift's rules for a new preacher are still valuable. His *Letter to a Young Gentleman about to be Ordained* (1721) is good advice for anyone learning or teaching the craft of preaching and sermon preparation. He says that a first essential is practice and a good English style should be cultivated. He explains, "Proper words in proper places, make the true definition of a style." He condemned the use of professional jargon arguing that simplicity must be maintained so that even the most unlearned may understand enough of what is said to be helpful to him. He thought it unreasonable of clergy to expect that the common man should understand expressions which are never used in common life. He said, "a Divine has nothing to say to the wisest congregation of any parish in this Kingdom which he may not say in a manner to be understood by the meanest among them."

The final quote shows something of the wit and humour of Jonathan Swift:

> "Among all the neglects of preaching none is so fatal than that of sleeping in the house of God; a scorner may listen to truth and reason, and in time grow serious; an unbeliever may feel the pangs of a guilty conscience; one whose thoughts or eyes may wander among other objects may, by a lucky word, be called back to attention, but the sleeper shuts up all avenues to his soul; he is like the deaf adder, that hearkeneth not to the voice of the charmer, charm he ever so wisely. And we may preach with as good success to the grave that is under his feet."

Jonathan Swift will always be an inspiration to churchmen in his commitment to a social application and appreciation of the Gospel. There remains the tendency of Irish Christians, and Anglicans not least, to compartmentise themselves into the religious and the secular. To have the forms of faith in the order and worship of the church separated from their needs and attitudes in everyday living. They cocoon themselves in their comfortable nests and refuse to involve themselves in the world around them to an extent greater than the need to go out there to earn a living or perhaps play a game. This attitude of church people who are often comfortably middle class is contrary to the teaching and example of Jesus. It was condemned in the example and teaching of Jonathan Swift who still stirs the consciences of those who read him and those whose thinking has been affected by him.

Chapter 4

Thomas Percy
1729-1811

Thomas Percy, Bishop of Dromore for nearly thirty years, was Dean of Carlisle when he was appointed to the See. It seems that the Rev Dr Jeffrey Elkins was offered an Irish bishopric by the Earl of Carlisle, the Lord Lieutenant of Ireland, in 1780, but as chaplain to the Earl he expressed a preference for the Deanery of Carlisle if Percy were to be offered the Irish appointment in his stead and an exchange could be arranged. The offer was transferred to Percy and he agreed to go to Ireland when a vacancy occurred there. He was also informed that the Irish bishopric was worth less than £2000 a year four times his income at Carlisle.

He expected, for some reason, to be made Bishop of Killala but when he was summoned to London in March 1782 he was offered the diocese of Dromore. Percy was then fifty-four years of age with a well recognised reputation as a scholar and writer. His best known literary work was *Reliques of Ancient English Poetry* in which he recovered from obscurity, and preserved from oblivion, many beautiful remains of genius; supplying the deficiencies in some, that were fragments and detached stanzas, and forming them into a whole by congenial taste, feeling and imagination. Percy's religious publications included *The Song of Solomon, newly translated from the original Hebrew, with a Commentary and Annotations.* (1764); *A Sermon preached before the Sons of Clergy* at their Anniversary Meeting in St Paul's, May 11, 1769 and *Key to the New Testament*(1765).

But the piece of writing which appealed to people generally was his little ballad, *O Nancy wilt thou go with me*? It was addressed to Anne Goodriche, the love of his life, and before their marriage which lasted for forty years. Thomas Stott, the Dromore poet and linen manufacturer, said of her: "By none, throughout a long and happy life, Was she surpassed as mother, friend and wife."

The poem displays a main characteristic in Percy, sensitivity and deep personal commitment to what was important to him.

> O Nancy, wilt thou go with me,
> Nor sigh to leave the flaunting town?
> Can silent glen have charms for thee,
> The lowly cot and russet gown?

Thos: Dromore,

Born 1729 — Died 1811.

Published by Nichols and Son, March 31 1846.

No longer dressed in silken sheen,
No longer decked with jewels rare;
Say, canst thou quit each courtly scene
Where thou wert fairest of the fair?

Nancy, when thou'rt far away,
Wilt thou not cast a wish behind?
Say, canst thou face the parching ray,
Nor, shrink before the wintry wind?
Oh, can that soft and gentle mien,
Extremes of hardship learn to bear,
Nor, sad, regret each courtly scene
Where thou wert fairest of the fair?

Nancy, canst thou love so true,
Through perils keen with me to go?
Or, where thy swain mishap shall rue,
To share with him the pangs of woe?
Say, should disease or pain befall,
"Wilt thou assume the nurse's care,
Nor, wistful, those gay scenes recall
When thou wert fairest of the fair?

And when at last thy love shall die,
Wilt thou receive his parting breath?
Wilt thou repress each struggling sigh,
And cheer with smiles the bed of death?
And wilt thou o'er his breathless clay
Strew flowers, and drop the tender tear?
Nor, then, regret those scenes so gay
Where thou wert fairest of the fair?

Literateur

Percy's literary successes made him a valued member of the group, men of letters and the arts, who were named "The Literary Club" or sometimes as "Dr Johnston and Company." They included the lexicographer and wit, and Oliver Goldsmith, Edmund Burke, Joshua Reynolds and David Garrick. Samuel Johnston was involved briefly in a Percy writing commission when he took on himself to write a memoir of Goldsmith, a project on which Percy and the Rev Dr Thomas Campbell, the Ulster author, had been engaged for some time. Johnston abandoned the task when he was faced with copyright problems. After his death Campbell wrote the script from materials provided by Percy, but he himself died six years before it was published. It was the Rev Henry Boyd, Rector of Drumgath, Rathfriland, Co Down, who put the finishing touches to the work. Boyd was given his living by Percy on transfer from the South of Ireland where he had been resident uneasily through the Rebellion of 1798. In 1785 Boyd had published the first translation into English verse of Dante's *Inferno* and the work had brought him fame. Incidentally he had two sons, the Rev Hannington Elgee Boyd was Rector of Dromara, Co Down, 1810-1864, and Prebendary of Dromara in the Chapter of Dromore Cathedral; and the Rev Charles Boyd, Rector of Ballynahinch, Co Down, 1817-1873. They had incumbencies of 54 and 55 years respectively and died in the active ministry, H.E at 94 and Charles at 97. Regrettably they were reputed to be most unbrotherly in their relationships. The Rev George Bellett, curate of Magherahamlet, originally the Chapel of Ease of Dromara, in his *Life* (1821) speaks of the Rev Charles Boyd, of Ballynahinch, brother of the Rev H E Boyd, but not on speaking terms with him. Johnston expressed his opinion of Thomas Percy to his friend and biographer, James Boswell, 23rd April 1778:

> "He is a man very willing to learn and very able to teach; a man out of whose company I never go without learning something. I know that he vexes me sometimes, but 1 am afraid that it is by making me feel my own ignorance. So much extension of mind and so much minute accuracy of enquiry, if you survey your wide circle of acquaintance you will find so scarce, if you find it at all, that you will value Percy by comparison ... Percy's attention to poetry has given grace and splendour to his studies of antiquity."

Percy said of Johnston's opinion of him: "I would rather have this than degrees from all the universities of Europe. It will be for me, and my, children, and grandchildren." Such was the standing of Johnston among his contemporaries. Whilst Percy appears to have regarded authorship as inconsistent with his position as a dignitary of the church - his writings as a bishop were requested to be published without reference to his title - he encouraged writers by a literary circle which he gathered around him at Dromore. He was always especially anxious to encourage writers in Irish, for he deplored the lack of interest in Irish language and writing and literature at that time.

Birth

Thomas Percy was born on 13th April 1729 at Bridgnorth, Shropshire, the son of a grocer, and educated at Christ College, Oxford, In 1756 he became vicar of Easton, Maudit, Northamptonshire; 1765 Domestic

Chaplain to the Duke and Duchess of Northumberland. whose family name was Percies with whom he claimed a distant relationship; 1769 Chaplain-in-Ordinary to King George 111 and a Doctor of Divinity of Cambridge University, having been admitted a member of Emmanuel College; 1778 Dean of Carlisle. Before leaving for Ireland the Percys lost their only son who had died at Marseilles in April 1782. He had become consumptive while at Cambridge and had been sent abroad for his health. A worry of lesser kind confronted Percy when he reached his diocese for there the episcopal residence was far from ready for occupation. It had been contracted for by his predecessor, the Hon William de la Poer Beresford, who had been translated to Ossory. Percy was faced with a bill for £3,200 of which £1,200 had to be paid by the end of the year, as well as £200 for the patent, while he had received only £900 from his official income. He managed to cope somehow for by 1783 he was settled in to the See House and happy about it and its surroundings in the town of Dromore. And he was pleased with the "genteel and agreeable families who have shown us every mark of respectful attention." One of the genteel neighbours was the Countess of Moira, the remarkable daughter of the celebrated Countess of Huntingdon, whose influence on Anglicanism and Methodism in England was considerable. In Percy's early days in Ireland the country was relatively prosperous and developing, but by the end years of the century there was civil war and the loss of separate identity. The violent situation was most diagreeable to Percy now seventy years of age and beginning to suffer from failing eye sight. He was in Northumberlandshire in the summer of 1797 with is wife and unmarried daughter visiting the

Isteads, his daughter and son-in-law. But early in 1798 the Primate and Archbishop of Armagh, William Newcombe, summoned back those bishops who were absent from their dioceses and Percy returned alone to Dromore. F J Bigger records;

> "Lord Castlereagh went so far as to write to him that if he absented himself the See of Dromore would be vacant. This Percy could not afford to risk, for the benefice was a rich one, worth £3,500 a year, so he could write to his wife: 'when I look back on the humble prospects with which we entered into the married state forty years ago, and reflect on our present splendour and comforts, what gratitude we must feel."

Castlereagh was Chief Secretary for Ireland and Francis Joseph Bigger was the famous or infamous politician and eccentric friend of Charles Stewart Parnell. Bishop Percy was in Dublin in June 1798 when the rebellion broke out in the North and he received accounts of the Battle of Ballynahinch in his diocese described as the decisive battle of the Rebellion for it marked the end of the rising of the United Irishmen. His informant was the bishop's steward who also wrote to tell him, we brought home two of the pikes used by the rebels for to be put along with your Lordship's other curiosities. Perry's relationships with the other denominations in his diocese were excellent. He involved himself in any community or charitable project which was for the common good in ways when Protestant and Roman Catholic were sharing in efforts to alleviate the distress of the poor of all the churches. The site for the Roman Catholic Church in the town of Dromore was the gift of Bishop Percy. Father Mornan, the Catholic parish priest, a gifted linguist was a personal friend of the bishop. Their literary tastes meant that they had much in common. Murnan nearly lost his life at the gates of the Cathedral in '98 when he was attacked by a mob determined to lynch him. He was strung up on a tree when Mr Crane Brush, the captain of the Dromore yeomanry, who was also Percy's agent, and lived in the house which is now the rectory, saw what was happening from the window of his room while he was shaving. Rushing out razor in hand he cut down the priest and the mob fled. It was Brush who was to be responsible for the imprisonment in Dromore of Henry Monroe, the Lisburn leader of the rebels at Ballynahinch. He was said to have treated his prisoner kindly. But as captain of the yeomanry he had to take his prisoner to stand trial before the general at Hillsborough. He was found guilty of treason and hanged. The rebellion having been stamped out in December '98 Bishop Percy preached a thanksgiving sermon in Dromore Cathedral at which many dissenters were in attendance. He believed they had abandoned republicanism and were anxious to forget the rebellion. He was in favour or the Act of Union of 1800 and used his influence in support of it. Percy the reconciler was pleased that good relations had been restored among the churches, clergy and people. Thomas Robinson, the English painter, was an intimate friend of Percy. After Mrs Percy's death on 30th December 1806 Robinson painted an imaginary scene in which he showed the bereaved bishop listening to Thomas Stott, the local poet reading some verses. The painting was titled "Dromore Palace 1807". Gathered around were Percy's close friends, Henry Boyd, Thomas Robinson

R E L I Q U E S

OF

ANCIENT ENGLISH POETRY:

CONSISTING OF

Old Heroic BALLADS, SONGS, and other
PIECES of our earlier POETS,

(Chiefly of the LYRIC kind.)

Together with some few of later Date.

VOLUME THE FIRST.

DURAT OPUS VATUM

L O N D O N:

Printed for J. DODSLEY in Pall-Mall.
M DCC LXV.

These venerable antient Song-enditers
Soar'd many a pitch above our modern writers
With rough majestic force they mov'd the heart,
And strength and nature made amends for Art.

and his precocious son Romney, Arthur O'Neill the blind harpist whom Mrs Percy had befriended, the new curate of Dromore, H E Boyd with his favourite flute, Sir George Atkinson, the eminent physician who had attended Mrs Percy in her illness, Viscount Castlereagh and the Hon Edward Ward.

Death

Thomas Percy died on 30th September 1811 in the eighty-third year of his age and the thirtieth of his episcopate. He was buried in a vault in the aisle which he had added, largely at his own expense, to Dromore Cathedral. It is still described as "the Percy Aisle". There is a memorial to him on the wall there. Regent Bridge over the River Lagan at the Cathedral was built in the year of his death and a plaque on it records that this monument of their respect was placed by the inhabitants of the town in the thirtieth year of Bishop Percy's residence in the See. Thomas Stott, too, erected a monument of which the base remains by the bank of the river. Thomas Percy's library was purchased by the Earl of Caledon to adorn the great house he was having remodelled by John Nash at Caledon in Co Tyrone. The price agreed by the Rev Pierce Meade, Percy's son-in-law, was £975 a large sum in 1812. The library remained in Caledon, almost overlooked by scholars, until 1969, when it was brought to Queen's University, Belfast. A few books were sold in 1928 and some 120 retained by the family at the time of the sale to the Earl of Caledon are in the Bodlian Library, Oxford. The 1800 volumes in Belfast virtually represent the whole of the library. ERR Green, the Irish historian, says, "in a sense it is proper that his (Percy's) books should have remained in Ireland for he had adapted himself to the country and to its ways while retaining common sense and tolerance which are not always characteristic of its people."

Thomas Percy's name appears in a stone over the West Door of the Church of St John, Dromara. The inscription advises that the building was re-dedicated by him in 1811 after reconstruction. There, too, is the name of the rector, H.E.Boyd, who had been appointed to the incumbency in 1810. This episcopal act could well have been one of the bishop's last engagements. There are other relics of Percy in Dromore Cathedral. The glass case in the chancel contains a prayer-book presented by him to the church and in the vestry room there is a case which contains Percy's episcopal robes. My little inset on the stone above the door of St John's Church, Dromara, is an indication of my ministry of almost thirty years in that incumbency and of its close association with Dromore Cathedral over several centuries. As Rural Dean and later as a member of the Chapter I developed an interest in the diocesan cathedral to find that little of any size and value had been written about this historic foundation and its parish. Because history is largely biography I wrote profiles of a few of the bishops of the Diocese of Dromore whom I considered to be especially worthy of remembrance. They were published with illustrations in "The Leader" the weekly newspaper of Dromore and district. I had hoped that they would have encouraged an. historian to undertake a sizable work on the cathedral and the town with parish and diocesan support for the project but I have been disappointed. Perhaps I should not have been for an unhappy feature of this part of Co Down and the diocese of Dromore is the lack of material on its ancient parish churches. The surprise is that for generations each of them had an incumbent, several had also curates assistant, most of the clergy were reasonably well educated with a few classical scholars among them but they were rarely pen men. The fact that a few churches have recently published brief parish histories could mean that things promise to be better in the future.

Chapter 5

Richard Mant
1776-1848

A mong those who have adorned the Bench of Bishops of the Church of Ireland none more deservedly earned the respect of his colleagues, contemporaries and successors than Richard Mant, Lord Bishop of Down and Connor (1823-48) and Dromore (1842-48). In the period, which included the episcopate of Richard Mant, the populous Diocese of Down and Connor, comprised the County of Antrim and a considerable part of County Down. The remainder of County Down and a section of County Armagh were in the Diocese of Dromore. Bishop Mant had been translated from the diocese of Killaloe and Kilfenora for which he had been consecrated in 1820. The eldest son, and fifth child of the Rev Dr Richard Mant, he was born at Southampton on 12th February 1776, where his father, who had been Master of the Grammar School, was Rector of All Saints. His considerable scholastic achievements were almost to be expected when cognisance is taken of the fact that his father's no mean academic attainments were surpassed by those of his maternal great grandfather, Dr Joseph Bingham, renowned scholar and author. A relation too, was Dr Richard Pococke, who was successively Lord Bishop of Ossory and Meath and an academician of repute. The boy Richard Mant had his primary education from his father. At thirteen he enrolled in Winchester College and after four happy years there was admitted to Trinity College, Oxford, where he graduated BA in 1797 and MA 1801. He earned a reputation at college and university for his ability and industry and these led to his appointment as a Fellow of Oriel College, Oxford, described as a proper recognition of his scholastic achievements. At Oriel he won the Chancellor's Prize for an essay on "Commerce", the earnest of a literary taste and talent which was to make him well known and highly regarded as writer and poet. He took Holy Orders when he was made a deacon in 1803. Licensed as curate assistant to his father he combined parochial work with that of a travelling teacher. Later he became curate of Bruriton, Hampshire, and an itinerant tutor. His literary inclinations took expression when he had some sermons published, among them one titled, "Eight Rules of the Christian Life, addressed to "persons lately confirmed."

Mant moved as curate to the rural parish of Crawley but was soon back as his father's colleague at All Saints, Southampton. There he wrote an explanation/commentary on the catechism using the question and answer method, it was a familiar and easy guide to the church catechism. He married Miss Elizabeth Woods in 1804. The ceremony was performed by William Bishop, Fellow of Oriel, who was born in the same month as Mant with six days between them, and they had both been elected to fellowships in Oriel on the same day. They remained intimate friends until Bishop's death in 1847. The date of the wedding day was the same as that of his parents thirty-six years before. The marriage of Richard and Elizabeth lasted for forty-one years. It was said of Elizabeth Mant that she was "a woman of sincere and sober piety; a constant student of the Bible; a lover of the Church of England; a careful and tender mother, a true and trusty friend; and a kind and diligent helper of the poor and needy." Mant became Vicar of Coggleshall, Essex, on 2 May 1810. He found the place a hotbed of dissent with the sacrament of baptism the main subject of contention. He published two dialogues - one on the necessity of baptism and the other on the defence of infant baptism. This willingness to publish his views on controversial issues remained with Mant throughout his life to show him to be a man of courage and considered judgment. He developed early the ability to make a case, whatever the subject, in precise, pungent and proper literary forms.

Lecturer and Author
He had the distinction of being chosen to deliver the Brampton Lectures of 1812. As was customary they were

given in the Church of St Mary, Oxford, in the Lent and Easter terms. His subject was "An appeal to the Gospel, or an Inquiry into the Justice of the Charge alleged by Methodists, and other Objectors, that the Gospel is not preached by the National Clergy." The lectures were published in the same year and they proved to be of such interest that they went to a seventh edition in 1816. He had a request from the Archbishop of Canterbury, Charles Manners Sutton, that a copy be sent to him for presentation to Her Majesty the Queen. Mant, perhaps on the strength of the Brampton Lectures, was offered and accepted the post of Domestic Chaplain to the Archbishop. That meant his resignation from the incumbency of Coggleshall and removal to London and Lambeth. It was there that the Mants lost their first child, Richard, which loss affected the mother very grievously. Richard Mant shared a major literary task when in 1813 with the Rev George D'Oyley, Christ's College, Cambridge, and later Rector of Lambeth, they edited notes and commentary for the Family Bible published by the Society for Promoting Christian Knowledge. The work took four years. Mant became select preacher at Oxford in 1814, a position he held for a couple of years.

The sermons he preached there were published with the title "Academical Discourses" in 1816. He was appointed Vicar of the prestigious parish of St Botolph, Bishopsgate, London, in 1815, the year when he was awarded his DD. Later the vicarage of East Horsely, Surrey, was added and Mant found pleasure in the mix of pastoral work in city and country. At that time he had the assistance of two curates.

Prof. Mant.

Ireland

When he was asked by the Prime Minister, Lord Liverpool, in 1820 to consider an appointment to an Irish bishopric he was less than enthusiastic. His son and biographer was to say: "He would never have gone to Ireland, had he not been impelled, in the first instance, by a sense of duty." Before any announcement was made a former curate and valued friend of Mant when told of the suggested move said to him, "I do not congratulate you." To which Mant replied, "No, it is not a subject for congratulation." When the proposition came the proposed See was Waterford, but a translation filled that vacancy and Mant was offered Killaloe and Kilfenora. He was consecrated bishop on 30 April 1820 in Cashel Cathedral. The diocese was much less conveniently sited than Waterford. His episcopate began in an Ireland suffering one of its periodic times of violence and terrorism. There was much criminal activity in the diocese though characteristically Mant went about his business regardless and in safety while many of his clergy were less fortunate. One rector who lived only five miles from the See House was robbed and his glebe house burned to the ground.

Richard Mant was translated to Down and Connor Diocese on 22 March 1823. The transition from a southern country diocese to a north-eastern one showing signs of quick industrial growth was a change much more than that of location but Mant's varied background and knowledge of urban and rural parishes was to stand him in good stead. When he arrived Down and Connor had no house for the bishop and he had to make his own living arrangements. Quickly he determined to procure a suitable residence. He did that after he persuaded Lord

Liverpool to provide the purchase money. The episcopate of Richard Mant was marked by his determination to have the church accommodate to the needs of its people. A first example of this concern was the founding of the "Free Church" named Christ Church, Belfast. It was to serve those who were not catered for sufficiently in other churches with their pew rents and a welcome for those who paid their dues.

The Free Church
The Marquis of Donegal provided the site, valued at £400; the Board of First Fruits granted £2000, and subsequently an additional £500, conditionally on a sum being raised by subscriptions; £1500 was raised by the efforts of the rector of the parish and the bishop made a gift of £100. Mant often did this when a new church was dedicated in his diocese. Christ Church was consecrated on 25th July 1833 and the seating capacity was for 1600 persons "without restrictions."   It became famous as a preaching place in the incumbencies of Dr Thomas Drew, the first rector, and his successor Dr Richard Rutledge Kane. They were Protestant apologists constantly attacking the Church of Rome for "its errors and false doctrine." It was Dr Drew who invited in a letter in a newspaper the nobility, gentry, clergy and laity to a meeting in Christ Church on 19th December 1838. It was the only church building in the city sufficiently large to accommodate the nearly 2000 people who were to attend it. The purpose of the meeting having been made known- to consider the future of the diocese and its needs in church buildings. The bishop who had asked that the meeting be held, explained the position as he saw it and pleaded his case so successfully that the decision was

taken to found "The Down and Connor Church Accommodation Society." In the five years of its existence - it was, wound up voluntarily in 1843 - £32000 was contributed and spent in building new churches, re-building, some old ones and improving and furnishing others. The society was most fortunate in having the services gratuitously of Charles Lanyon, one of the most talented architects of his day, in the designs of new buildings and for proposals on how to proceed with other projects. Mant encouraged other benefactors to the extent that he had gifts of sites for sixteen churches, donations of furniture and fittings and Holy Communion Plate. Mant went to the House of Lords, in his turn, in 1825 but he found the chamber so little to his taste that he gladly left what went on at Westminster to others. Bishop Mant was an apologist for Anglicanism and his work is seen in that field when he replied to Lord Melbourne who resented the intention to have an Anglican mission to Roman Catholics for the reason that "the main opinions of that church being essentially the same as our own."

Mant published a *Letter to Lord Melbourne* in January 1836, titled *Does the Church of Rome agree with the Church of England in all the Fundamentals of Christianity? - answered by the autoritative Declarations of both Churches.* He described what Melbourne had said as "an arbitrary and baseless assumption, and irreconcilable with historical, recorded, and indisputable facts." The encounter with Melbourne was an example of Mant's championing of Anglicanism and his ability as a most competent debator in the Roman Catholic/Anglican controversy. The suggestions of the Anglican And

Roman Catholic Commission, April 1982, apparently insufficiently considered the differences between Romanism and Anglicanism in their search for a unity which is bound to be elusive because the divisive beliefs and practices remain. Richard Mant's strong attacks on Roman Catholicism appeared in two pamphlets, *The Churches of Rome and England Compared* and *Romanism and Holy Scripture Compared.*

Missional Council

The Bishop was involved with the redoubtable Protestant and Orange Institution champion, the Rev Dr Thomas Drew, in the foundation of the Diocesan Home Mission Council, 31 August 1836. Other societies which had Mant's sympathy and support were founded or strengthened in his episcopate. They included the Clergy Aid Society, the Church Education Society and the Additional Curates Society for Ireland. He wrote another pamphlet in 1837 on *Extemporaneous Prayer, not authorised by the Church in her public service.* It was a reply, and a contrary judgment, to those who found in the 55th English canon permission for extempore prayer in the pulpit while demanding prescribed form for the prayer desk. "The prayer desk bound the pulpit free," but Mant would have none of it. In a closely reasoned argument he dealt with the weaknesses of extempore prayer and the strengths of ordered forms and advocated the disciplined use of the latter at all times.

Dromore

Richard Mant became Bishop of Dromore in 1842 on the death of James Saurin, who was to be the last bishop in its singularity of that diocese. Saurin was a Belfastman son of the Rev James Saurin, Vicar of Belfast, and brother of the celebrated Attorney-General Saurin. The Diocese of Dromore was joined with that of Down and Connor and thus an arrangement was resumed which had been in being in the episcopate of Jeremy Taylor. The United Dioceses of Down, Connor and Dromore remained until the separation of Connor from the others in 1945. In his first visitation of the clergy of Dromore Diocese, Mant gave them a Charge which he had given previously to those of Down and Connor. It was published as a pamphlet entitled, *The Laws of the Church, the Churchman's Guard against Romanism and Puritanism.* He warned against a partiality to the latter because of a distrust of the former. He spoke against "an undue tendency towards Geneva" so that in the height of our disapprobation and alarm at the one , we may be drawn aside to take friendly counsel with the other. The Bishop had a total commitment to his own church and was convinced of its place and purpose in the Christian economy. It seems incredible that someone who had distinguished himself as an opponent of Roman Catholicism should be charged with having Romish tendencies but that is what happened. The charges came because of his efforts to obtain liturgical conformity in his diocese. A cause of the dissention was Mant's support of the Church Architectural Society with its programme of "innovations." He finished with a personal plea for better understanding of himself, as their bishop, and his associates with:

> "We have no secrets to conceal; there is no inspection from which we shrink: But do not condemn us on partial representations, unseen, unheard, and unknown."

The writings of Mant on Roman Catholicism remain essential reading for anyone who is concerned to compare it with Anglicanism. This must be the case even though there have been many changes in Roman Church attitudes and practices since the Second Vatican Council and subsequently.

Bereavement

Mrs Mant who had suffered long from rheumatic gout and was often confined to her bedroom passed away peacefully while they were visiting their eldest son at Hillsborough, County Down. The date was 2nd April 1845. Walter Bishop Mant had been appointed Archdeacon of Down in 1834 on the death of his uncle Archdeacon Richard Mullins Mant. The death of Elizabeth was an irreparable loss to a man whose dependence on his wife was patent for all to see. He never reconciled himself to living without her. Her loss burdened his soul until his death. Archdeacon Berens described the final year:

> "In the summer of 1848, Bishop Mant, for a short time, took a lodging in Oxford, and afterwards allowed himself the melancholy satisfaction of visiting Southampton, and Bruriton and other places in Hampshire and Sussex, which were endeared to him by the recollection of early happiness. Upon his return to Ireland he engaged in the fulfilment of his Episcopal duties with his wonted zeal and energy. On 12th September he completed a tour of Confirmations, in the County of Down - his seventh general tour in 25 years. He held an Ordination on the 24th of the same

month; consecrated a church on the 26th; and presided at three important meetings of the Society for the Propagation of the Gospel in Foreign Parts, on the three following days."

He visited his sister, Mrs Phillot, until 27th October when he felt languid and weak. He was suffering from erysipelas and low fever. There was to be no recovery. He had no pain just weakness and sinking rapidly he resigned his spirit without a struggle or a sigh. He died on 2 November 1848. His death was a grievous loss to his family, and to the church which he had served selflessly, proudly and with great distinction. His son writing to a friend said: "It is a satisfaction to us, however, that he has been removed without any tedious, painful or wasting disease, but (till within a few hours of his death) in full vigour of mind, and activity of body for his age. He had been mercifully spared the endurance of BLINDNESS, which was approaching from a cataract, and which, I think, he dreaded. His labours are over, and he is, I trust, gone to his reward."

Poet and Author
Richard Mant earned reputations as preacher, author, and administrator; and as poet and hymnist. His poetry had a fine humanity about it, coming as it does from tributes to people, and expressions of faith and feelings. He wrote this poem in grateful recollection of his father's care for him and the good tuition and training he had given him.

Yet, O my father, I can ne'er forget,
Nor e'er, remembering, cease to feel the debt
To thee lowe; nor e'er that debt repay;

To the last evening of my mortal day.
Thou gav'st me being, sweeter far than this,
Thou gav'st me that, which makes my being bliss,
Thou did'st to holy thoughts my bosom warm,
Thou did'st my tongue to holy accents form,
And teach, in dawning season's infant days,
To lisp the voice of prayer, and thanks and praise.

He wrote in verse to his fiancée:
"Whence sprang the wish with thee to share
My every joy, my every care;
And tread with thee, my lowly way,
Till evening close our peaceful day."

In a tribute to his friend, William Bishop, he said:
"And he of meek simplicity, the child,
Strict to himself, to others' failings blind;
Servant of heaven, and friend of human kind;
For twice ten years his guileless heart I've known,
Nor mark'd a thought which angels might not own."

He produced a metrical version of the Psalms. His version of the Twenty-third Psalm was:

My shepherd is the Lord most high;
His care shall all my wants supply;
Lay in pastures green to feed,
And to the tranquil streamlet lead,

He shall my erring soul reclaim,
In honour of his holy name;
And teach me when my steps would stray,

To keep the straight and even way.

Though through the gloomy vale I tread,
Of death no evil shall I dread;
For Thou art ever at, my side
Thy staff to guard Thy rod to guide,

My plenteous board shalt Thou dispose,
In spite of my reluctant foes;
With oil shalt Thou anoint my brow,
And make my brimmed cup o'erflow.

Abundant goodness, deathless love,
Shall on my steps attendant move,
Nor length of days my fix'd abode
Shall sever from the House of God.

As a hymnwriter, Mant's spiritual songs are fine examples of the genre, and one of them "Bright the vision that delighted" is among the most used by Irish Anglicans. We have two others in the Church Hymnal, "See the destined day arise" and "For all thy saints, O Lord."

Charges
Mant's Episcopal Visitations and Charges to his clergy are interesting documents and so forthright in their views that it is not surprising they caused angry reactions at times. The plain speaking was allied to Mant's ambitions; which were aimed at producing high standards in faith and practice from his clergy and which he illustrated in his own conduct. They could be prescribed reading for clergy in these very different days.

Many of the themes are still relevant and all of them are treated with sensitivity and such a sense of shared responsibilty, Bishop and Pastor, that they encourage and persuade to views of ministry which are lofty and Christ-like. At a Primary Visitation in Lisburn on 4th July 1824 he commented on the Holy Scriptures,

> "They should be the first object of our attention. As they are the source from which all our doctrine is to be drawn, the touchstone to which all our teaching is to be referred, so that they be the perpetual scope of our pursuits, the perpetual companion of our thoughts;"

They form indeed an ample treasure house of learning; and they who have penetrated into it most deeply, and examined it most perfectly, are best aware how precious, how abundant, how inexhaustible are its stores. They deserve, as they demand, a large portion of a Clergyman's time."

He went on to emphasise the requirements of the Ordinal in this subject. He drew attention to political controversies in his Ordinary Visitation at Lisburn on 3 August 1825. He said:

> "They frequently interfere very materially with the harmony and comfort of society; especially to those struggles of rival and conflicting parties which on particular occasions are apt to arise, to the infinite detriment of all kindly feeling, good order and tranquillity, in the districts which are the scene of the contest. The Clergyman indeed is a citizen as well as a

churchman; he is a member of the state as well as a minister of the church; he has civil rights to preserve, as well as religious duties to perform. True. Yet it is easy to perceive which is his distinctive, and which ought to be his predominant character. It were more difficult, I think, to show, that that zeal is according to spiritual knowledge which prompts him to engage in contentions, scenes which are notoriously calculated to cause those, who heartily engage in them, to make shipwreck concerning charity: or which at least afford occasion for much temporary confusion, and excite a spirit of discord and mutual animosity, wherewith charity can hardly consist. Surely the eagerness of a political partisan is an unseemly appendage to the character of one, who is pledged to maintain and set forward quietness, peace and love, among all Christian people nor do the artifices of a political intriguer more properly become one, who is equally pledged to draw all his cares and studies the way of his sacred profession and to give up the study of the world and the flesh. This caution applies in common to all the clergy of the united church, who may be exposed to the temptation of taking active parts in political controversies."

There were many political parsons in Mant's time. It would appear that his good and wholesome advice was not taken by them.

History

A prolific writer - Mant's mind and pen were never idle - his major work at least in size was his two volume *History of the Church of Ireland.* The work deals with the periods from the Reformation to the Revolution and from the Revolution to the Act of Union. Much of it was written in Dublin in the spring of 1839. His son and biographer, the Venerable Walter Bishop Mant said of them:

> "They are distinguished by the deep and patient research which characterise all his weightier writings; and many even of his lesser ones; they give an accurate and trustworthy account of important events, and contain much curious information not readily found elsewhere; and bear the impress of a mind which thoroughly understood, and a heart which intensely loved, the excellences of the Church of which he was a chief minister, and whose trials, and difficulties, and labours he had undertaken to delineate."

The judgment of the son has been echoed by many who have made use of the work of a writer to whom the Church of Ireland will always be indebted.

Chapter 6

William Alexander
1824-1911

Willliam Alexander was one Church of Ireland bishop who was Irish born. Irish Sees had often been filled with English clerics, some of them like Jeremy Taylor, Thomas Percy and Richard Mant added lustre to the church of their adoption. There were others whose contribution was minimal. Alexander was born on 13 April 1824 the son of the Rev Robert Alexander, Rector of Termoneeny, and later of Errigal, Garvagh and Aghadowey, Diocese of Derry. Robert's uncle was Nathaniel Alexander, Bishop of Meath. The Alexanders were like many notable Anglo-Irish families of the period with church and army connections. They were kin to the Alexanders of Caledon, Co Tyrone, and the earls of that designation. The famous 1939-1945 war soldier, Field-Marshal Earl Alexander of Tunis was one of them. And there were Royal Navy connections, too, for from another branch of the family came Admiral Henry McClintock Alexander.

As a boy William Alexander had difficulty with the movement of his legs so that Charles James Lever, the medical doctor and novelist, diagnosed the dreaded hip disease. The treatment of the complaint put him to bed on his back for twelve months. In age, when lameness compelled him to walk with the aid of a stick he often spoke of his childhood illness as though to explain his weakness. He was greatly influenced by his parents in his youth - his mother, nee Dorothea McClintock, and his father were second cousins - and by his paternal grandmother whose enthusiasm for good literature rubbed off on her grandson. She was also a deeply committed Protestant.

He had the benefit of the friendship of his father's curates. One of them was especially helpful, to him, Thomas Rolleston, who was a fine classical scholar. The influence of family and friends encouraged him to study for the ministry of the church. Like other sons of the clergy at the time he was educated in England at Tonbridge School and at Oxford University from which he graduated BA in 1847. He was ordained in Muff Church, County Donegal, on 19 September 1847 by the Honourable Richard Ponsonby Bishop of Derry and Raphoe, for the curacy of Templemore of which the Cathedral, Londonderry, was the parish church. His rector was John Bunbury Gough, Dean of Derry, and brother of the famous Viscount Gough. The dean's sons John and Tom were soldiers and Benjamin was a clergyman. It was Ben Gough who introduced William Aleaander to Fanny Humphries who lived since she was fifteen years old at Milltown House, Strabane. Her father was agent to the Duke of Abercorn and a landowner in his own right.

The courtship William and Fanny was a short one and the marriage supremely happy. It was solemnised on 15 October 1850 in the old parish church of Strabane, long since demolished. His first incumbency was the parish of Termonamongan, near Castlederg, County Tyrone. In his student and beginning days of ministry Alexander was much influenced by John Henry Newman who was to become the never really happy convert to Roman Catholicism. Newman's secession to the Church of Rome though it shocked Alexander it did nothing to doubt his belief in the truth of Anglicanism. Newman was the first apologist of the Oxford Movement. Its chief object was the defence of the Church of England as a Divine Institution, of the doctrine of Apostolic Succession and of the Book of Common Prayer as the rule of faith. Its tracts titled *Tracts for the Times* were written for this purpose. Alexander's interest in the Oxford Movement could well have been a response to the sermon preached by the Rev John Keble in the University Church at Oxford in 1833 against the suppression of ten Irish bishoprics by Act of Parliament. The sermon and the response to it marked the beginning of the Oxford Movement. It determined to restore High Church principles; to reverse the decline in church life and to oppose the spread of "Liberalism" in theology which was fast gaining ground in the Church of England. Its leaders were John Keble, John Henry Newman and Edward Bouverie Pusey. Keble (1792-1866) was Professor of Poetry at Oxford and Pusey (1850-82) was Professor of Hebrew there while Newman (1801-90) was Vicar of St Mary's, Oxford. The members of the Movement were called Tractarians because they published *Tracts for the Times* from 1833-41. At first these were brief leaflets but later they were learned treatises. The leaders were their authors and Newman wrote twenty-four of them himself. It was his tract Number 90, an interpretation of the Thirty-nine Articles of Religion which appeared to make them agreeable with the decrees of the Roman Catholic Church's Council of Trent. The tract caused such a storm of protest that it brought the series to an end. While the Oxford Movement had considerable support among church people it was always faced with fierce attack from liberals in the university and the Bishops. It was grievously affected when a party within advocated submission to the Church of Rome. After the censure by the Convocation of Oxford in 1845 of a book by W G Ward and again after the Gorham case in 1850, there were a number of conversions to the RC Church. But the majority remained in the C of E, and despite the hostility of the press and the Government, the movement spread. Its influence was exercised in the sphere of worship and ceremonial, in the social sphere (the slum settlements were among its notable achievements), and in the restoration of the religious life in the C of E.

William George Ward (1812-82) theologian and philosopher, was a fellow of Balliol College. He was deprived of his degrees for heresy and later became a Roman Catholic. The Gorham Case of 1847 caused much controversy. G C Gorham, an evangelical clergyman, had been refused institution to a cure because the Bishop of Exeter, H Fhilpotts, ruled him to be doctrinally unsound because of his interpretation of what is meant by baptismal regeneration. After protracted legal proceedings Gorham won the case and in 1851 was instituted to his benefice. It was the refusal of the Church of England to enforce the Roman Catholic doctrine of Baptism that caused the Tractarians, Archdeacons Manning and Wilberforce to secede from it and to join the Church of Rome. H E Manning was to become the Cardinal Archbishop of Westminster. It was he who tried to prevent 78 years old Newman from being made a cardinal. His duplicity backfired and Newman was honoured by the Pope and allowed to remain at his Birmingham Oratory "against the rules." Fanny Alexander had also been influenced by the Oxford Movement - John Keble had written the preface to her first book of hymns in 1847 for she had theological perceptions and a developed sense of the importance of Christian dogma. Like her husband she combined successfully the theological and the practical and while naturally shy and introverted she was a dedicated honorary social worker in the years while the country struggled to get over the effects of the "Great Hunger", caused by the potato famine. Fortunately it was less severe in her part of the country. Much of her poetry has a strong social content to it. An incident from those early years showed that the poetess had married a poet. William composed an ode to the Earl of Derby for an Oxford speech day and described how he did it.

“I chose an early day and a distant parochial call
not far from Pettigo for the colligation in verse

of my scattered thoughts, the binding of my stalks into one sheaf of measure."

He explained how it was sent for competition: "It was copied out by my Fanny in her exquisite writing, and sent in to the University Registrar."
The poem and its recitation by Alexander in the theatre of Oxford made a deep and lasting impression on the learned audience. William Alexander became Rector of Upper Fahan on the shores of Lough Swilly in 1855 and in 1860 of Camus-juxta-Mourne (Strabane) the most valuable living in the dioceses of Derry and Raphoe. He was made Dean of Emly in 1863, a merely titular dignity which did not entail any change of residence. He had become well known as preacher and speaker on both sides of the channel. His engagements brought the Alexanders many friendships like that with Bishop Samuel Wilberforce and his brother-in-law H E Manning, when Archdeacon of Chichester. William and Fanny were on intimate terms with some of the great religious and literary personalities of the time and with others whose names were well known in British public life. As a contributor to *The Speaker's Commentary* he was the colleague of the theologians Lightfoot, Westcott, Howson, Rawlinson and Plumtre.

Alexander was a candidate for the Professorship of Poetry at Oxford and Matthew Arnold was especially anxious for his appointment, but he was defeated by Sir Francis Doyle. When he was appointed Bishop of Derry Doyle said that he was sure Alexander would make a much better bishop than he would. Archbishop Magee's biographer writing about a York Congress and referring to the capability of Alexander said:

"Magee followed the Dean of Emly - whose great powers as an orator would have thrown any other speaker into the shade."

Alexander had the distinction of being the Select Preacher at Oxford in 1870, 1872, 1882, 1907; at Cambridge in 1872, 1892 and at Dublin in 1879. He was the Bampton Lecturer in 1876 on "The Witness of the Psalms to Christ and Christianity." He preached sermons on special set subjects at St Margaret's, Westminster, and St Peter's, Piccadilly. W E Gladstone, the politician, and W E H Lecky, the historian and essayist, were sometimes in his congregations. It was said that those who thought deeply, or spoke or wrote, sooner or later went to hear him. His sermons at Westminster Abbey and St Paul's Cathedral made a deep impression on many who listened to them. He delivered orations on Jeremy Taylor and John Milton which were notable for their painstaking research and the perceptiveness of their insights into the contributions to religion and literature of these two most capable and remarkable men. He wrote sensitively and spoke feelingly on that complex character Thomas Ken whose hymns "Sun of my soul, Thou Saviour dear" and "Glory to Thee, my God this night" are still sung by church people. Alexander's first preaching engagement at Westminster Abbey was in 1867. It was while he was in London for that engagement that he heard of the death of his diocesan, Dr William Higgin, Bishop of Derry and Raphoe. He was embarrassed when the death having been published he was named by the London paper, "The Owl," as the likely successor. It was to be proved right though it had been no foregone conclusion for Magee,

Dean of Cork, and Lee, Archdeacon of Dublin, had been short listed with him.

Alexander would not have been the choice of the Derry and Raphoe diocesan clergy who knew him well and considered him to be too young for the episcopate in times when dignity and long service were regarded as essentials in a bishop. It must have been touch and go for Disraeli favoured Magee and he had the ear of the Prime Minister, Lord Derby. It was Alexander's socalled "High Church" views which made him suspect too many influential people so that it showed courage in those who brought about his appointment. The intimation of his election was brought to Alexander by the Duke of Abercorn, Lord Lieutenant of Ireland, on behalf of the Queen.

He was consecrated in St Patrick's Cathedral, Armagh on Sunday 6th October 1867 at 43 years of age. It was a matter of some historical interest that this was the first consecration of a Bishop of Derry in Armagh Cathedral since the Reformation. Bishops, especially to the best endowed Sees, used to be sent to Ireland ready-made. He received his Doctor of Divinity degree from Trinity College Dublin in 1867. Whether the new bishop or the people of his diocese changed or both accommodated to each other it was a short time until he was well accepted everywhere. The bishops of England and Ireland had expressed their pleasure at his election to the episcopate. The voice of the Bishop of Derry was a strong one in the debates on the Disestablishment of the Church of Ireland. He was heard with sympathy by Gladstone but no one was to be allowed to stay the passing of the Act of Disestablishment. The feelings of church people were at once regretful and hopeful. There was regret at the ending of a 700 years link with the state which had been seen as of mutual benefit to church and country; and hope that the change would mean new freedom for the church with its recovery of its ancient independence. Mrs Alexander in her hymn which was sung at church services on 1st January 1871 expressed the feelings of those who were unable to see any good in the upheaval which Disestablishment would bring in its train.

> Look down, Lord of Heaven,
> on our desolation
> Fallen, fallen, fallen is now
> our country's crown,
> Dimly draws the New Year
> on a churchless nation,
> Ammon and Amalek tread
> our borders down,
> Lord, we have sinned.
> Kneeling down before Thee
> Make we full confession,
> the people and the priest.
> In our day of plenty little fruit
> we bore Thee,
> Oh, the fast forgotten!
> Oh, the songless feast!

The bishop was awarded an honorary DCL degree by Oxford University in 1876 and an LLD TCD in 1892. In 1891 William Alexander was the guest of the Bishop of New York for an American visit which allowed him to meet President Harrison at Washington and Phillips Brooks in Boston. There he met with Brooks the incredible Helen Keller when she was 12 yrs old and in whom the celebrated preacher was showing an interest. He visited South Africa in 1893 with daughter Eleanor as his travelling companion, for Fanny was too ill to travel such long distances. Mrs Alexander died on 12 October 1895 aged 77 to the great grief of her husband, the family and everyone who knew her. William was totally devastated. In life she had helped him, for without her his most ardent admirer must admit that he would have been a lesser man. Years later William Alexander said of their marriage,

> "Perfect union is very rare; it is not possible, when men may think in moments of folly, without oneness of soul like hers and mine. That must outline all meaner emotions."

William Alexander was elected Archbishop of Armagh and Primate of All Ireland by his brother bishops in February 1896 - four months after Fanny's death - and enthroned in the Cathedral, Armagh, on 24 March 1896 at 72 years of age and after twenty-nine years as Bishop of Derry and Raphoe. He succeeded Archbishop Gregg who had held the primacy for only two years. Among those who were delighted with Alexander's appointment was William Johnston of Ballykilbeg, the Orange Institution's folk hero whose principles had been so strong that he had suffered imprisonment for them, and who was therefore the better able to appreciate unswerving principle in another. And it was as administrator as well as preacher that Alexander made an impression on the Church of Ireland and the whole Anglican Communion. His well considered judgments and sense of values made it necessary to take careful note of everything he said. He had a special interest in the building of St Anne's Cathedral, Belfast, ,for he insisted that the future of his church was bound up with its progress in the North- East corner of the island, He was an enthusiastic ecumenist in that he wanted union among the Protestant churches. He earned the esteem of those of other communions for his understanding of their problems. The degree DLitt was conferred on him by Oxford University in 1907 and he was admitted an Honorary Fellow of Brasenose College, Oxford, also in 1907. He received the GCVO in 1911, a Royal recognition which gave pleasure to a great many people. At his resignation in 1910 there was a fine tribute to him from the Bench of Bishops which ended: "As we part with so much genius and so much charm, we earnestly pray to our Heavenly Father to be with our father and friend in his honourable and honoured retirement, to sustain his aged footsteps, and to make his pillow smooth." Alexander had been a diocesan bishop for forty-three years. He made his retirement home at Torquay and for' the short time left to him he enjoyed the delights of a part of England steeped, in history and famed for its scenery. There was the place where William of Orange landed when he came to receive the Crown of England and where a statue was erected to mark the event. There, too, is the house where Henry Francis Lyte wrote his immortal hymn, "Abide with me."

No testimony to the work and worth of William Alexander was more tender, more sincere and more worthy than that contained in a letter to him from Randall Davidson, Archbishop of Canterbury.

My Dear Lord Primate,

I have purposely waited until the date of your actual resignation drew nigh before writing to you to express my own sense of loss which the whole church sustains in your laying down at length the burden of high office and responsibility which you have borne so long. It is always a grand thing when the bearer of one of our highest offices is a man who by his gifts adds lustre to the position he holds - gifts, I mean which lie outside the NECESSARY range of qualifications. And I am quite certain that the Church of Ireland, at a time of peculiar difficulty, has stood forth before the world in a clearer light because she has been presided over by a man of independent genius, of high poetic power, and of literary and oratorical eminence such as yours. We have all sat at your feet time after time, and have learned, with a mixture of envy, admiration, and despair, to look on, from below, at the output of a teaching and inspiring force such as few have been privileged to wield. And when to all this is added the beneficent force of deep spiritual teaching and the example of a noble personal life, the gain is of the sort which uplifts not the Church of Ireland only; but the Anglican Church throughout the world. Ever since as an undergraduate at Oxford I listened to the Bishop of Derry and went back to my rooms to write down some recollection of his words, I have looked to your words, written and spoken, for help and guidance. And I pray God that we may yet be allowed in the coming years to draw

courage and inspiration from the fount which has refreshed and stimulated us so long. That every highest and deepest and most Holy blessing from on High may rest upon you in the eventide of life is the prayer of your
Affectionate and grateful,

Randall Cantuar.
Lambeth Palace, 29 January 1911.

Part of the national tribute to Primate Alexander was a portrait by Mr Harris-Brown for the National Gallery of Ireland. While it is probable that men who in every walk of life impress their personalities on their fellows owe much to their ladies William Alexander's wife was a partner of exceptional worth. She had talents and abilities which complemented his own and her knowledge of and enthusiasm for the faith was so clearly illustrated in her poems and hymns that some esteemed her more highly than they did her husband.

It is often the fate of writers and composers that though their works are well known they are unknown to people generally.

It is somewhat different with Mrs Cecil Frances Alexander who is known as the writer of one of the best known hymns ever written, "There is a green hill far away." She wrote some 400 hymns and poems and some of them are nearly as well known as "The green hill." Her hymns were written for purposes. The three most famous "Hymns for Little Children" occur among the fourteen composed to explain the articles of the Apostles' Creed. "All things bright and beautiful" ("Maker of heaven and earth"); "Once in royal David's city" ("Who was conceived by the Holy Ghost born of the Virgin Mary") "There is a green hill far away" ("Suffered under Pontius Pilate, was crucified, dead and buried") are examples of her method. Her versification of St Patrick's Breastplate - "I bind unto myself today /The strong name of the Trinity" - is much appreciated by many more than Irish Christians.

It was first sung in procession at the enthronement of William C Magee as Archbishop of York in York Minster. Her poem "The Burial of Moses" has been described as "the finest sacred lyric in the English language." The American entertainer, Mark Twain, often recited it in full to appreciative audiences. Here are two verses of it.

By Nebo's lonely mountain,
On this side Jordan's wave,
In a vale in the 'land of Moab
There lies a lonely grave.
And no man knows that sepulchre,
And no man saw it e'er,
For the angels of God upturned the sod,
And laid the dead man there.

And had he not high honour,
The hillside for a pall,
To lie in state, while angels wait
With stars for tapers tall,
And the dark rock pines, like tossing plumes,
Over his bier to wave,
And God's own hand in that lonely land
To lay him in the grave.

A narrative poem which thrilled loyalist Ulstermen and titled "The Siege of Derry" has the verses:

'Twas the Lord who gave the word when his people drew the sword

For the freedom of the present, for the future that awaits.

Child thou must remember that bleak day in December

When the 'Prentice Boys of Derry rose up and shut the gates.

There was tumult in the street, and a rush of many feet

There was discord in the Council, and Lundy turned to fly,

For the man had no assurance of Ulstermen's endurance,

Nor the strength of him who trusted in the arm of God Most High.

Then those Derry men shall tell-who would serve his country well,

Must be strong in his conviction and valiant I in his deed,

Must be patient in enduring, and determined in securing

The liberty to serve his God, the freedom of his creed.

Mrs Alexander is more than a name for many could add the information that she was the wife of a Church of Ireland Bishop of Derry and Raphoe. They might add that she wrote her most famous hymn as she sat in her window overlooking the Walls of Derry and the hill beyond, and thought of that other walled city and

Calvary's Hill and its consequences for all mankind because of what happened there. Like many another good story it is fiction, for the hymn was written years before she came to live in Londonderry. And yet like all good fiction it has a deal of truth in it, for it is likely that Cecil Frances Alexander, knowing the city and its environs well, did make the comparison with Jerusalem and Calvary. For a lady who lacked nothing in imagination and sensitivity the application would be easy enough. When Archbishop J A F Gregg showed Mr Maude, the statesman, around the Primate's palace at Armagh in 1946 with its portraits of his predecessors and they looked one of Mrs Alexander which was there, too. Maude remarked on how good it was to have her in the collection. Gregg said,

> "Perhaps she is more famous than any other here. She is known by her hymns all the world over. She may well have had a greater influence than any Primate."

Canon G W O Addlesham, sometime Dean of Chester, had a similar experience.

> "When I remarked (to Gregg) upon the wonderful grasp of theology that comes out of her (Mrs Alexander's) hymns, he said that in her day there was an understanding of theology among the educated laity which is very rare nowadays."

Because of the partnership of the Alexanders and her well recognised literary attainments it seems reasonable and appropriate that she should be included by the side of her husband in this profile of him.

Chapter 7

William Shaw Kerr
1873-1960

Among the reasons I have for penning this profile of the former Church of Ireland Bishop of Down and Dromore is that he made me a deacon in St Clement's Church, Templemore Avenue, Belfast, on 26th June, 1949, where I was to serve a curacy with Canon WHN Fisher, and ordained me a priest in St Mark's Church, Newtownards, on 24th June 1950. The more compelling one is that he earned a good reputation as theologian, historian and Anglican apologist. William Shaw Kerr has left us more than memories in books which remain valuable repositories of theological and historical research, of information and clarification on matters of continuing interest and importance to us. My look here is less at the person and the parson, more at the penman who made his contribution to religion and life in this country. William Shaw Kerr was a man of many parts - scholar, historian, polemicist, educationalist and ecumenist. His writings alone made him distinctive from his peers. And he was his own man taking up positions in church and society different to others, and always for well argued and carefully articulated reasons.

Birth

He was born in Wicklow, 25 July, 1873, and after first level studies, he distinguished himself with his academic successes at Trinity College, Dublin. He was ordained for the curacy of Shankill, Lurgan, 1897-99; and was curate in St James, Belfast, 1899-01; and successively rector of Ballywalter, 1901-10; St Paul's, Belfast, 1910-15; and Seapatrick, Banbridge, 1915-32. He was Archdeacon of Dromore, 1930-32; and Dean of Belfast, 1932-45 when on the 23 January he was consecrated Bishop of Down and Dromore in St Anne's Cathedral. As was the custom in those days TCD conferred on him an honorary Doctor of Divinity Degree. He retired 31 July 1955 and died 3 February 1960.

W S Kerr put his scholarship to good use in publications of particular value for the better understanding of Irish, and Irish Church, History. His *Independence of the Celtic Church in Ireland* (1931) remains essential reading for those who are concerned about the spurious claims of the Roman Catholic Church to a heritage which is properly that of the Church of Ireland. As a polemicist his major work, *A Handbook on the Papacy,* (1950) is a useful text book on Roman Catholicism, the system of papal government, and that church's claim to absolute truth. Again he makes the case for the legitimacy of the Irish Church and highlights the weaknesses and contradictions in Romish doctrine, practice and treatment of other churches. He defended George Walker who was being attacked for his alleged incompetences and misdemeanours at the Siege of Londonderry by a Presbyterian minister of his time, John McKenzie, and Presbyterian historians thereafter, in his *George Walker of Derry* (1938). And in response to Presbyterian charges against Jeremy Taylor and his fellow bishops for their treatment of co-religionists, he wrote *Who Persecuted: Episcopalian and Presbyterian in Ulster* (1947) a defence of the bishops and a clarification of the position of Presbyterian ministers holding incumbencies in the Church of Ireland and why they had to be removed from them.

Other publications included *The Worship of the Virgin Mary, Wages and Profits, A Memoir of the Life of the Rev Andrew Boyd* (1927) and he edited *A History of Banbridge*, (1936). His writings remain valuable repositories of theological, historical and sociological research, information and clarification, on matters of continuing importance in the understanding of people and problems which still have to be faced.

Kerr was a contributor to several journals and newspapers. He was never loath to express himself on matters of concern to church and state. He often took a liberal stance and robustly defended himself against others with contrary opinions. Because WS Kerr was the first Bishop of Down and Dromore, it is necessary to say something of the division of the diocese of Connor from that of Down and Dromore. It was occasioned by the population growth of Belfast. In 1871 it was 46,000 by

1911, 118,000 and growing rapidly. Clerical manpower had also increased and churches needed to be provided for the Church of Ireland percentage of the population in what was fast becoming a heavily industrialised city. The growth problem of Belfast was recognised throughout the Church of Ireland and in 1928 General Synod set up a commission empowered to make loans to assist in church building there. The initial move in the division of the dioceses to meet the developing situation was made at General Synod on 13th May 1925 on the proposal of Charles King Irwin, Archdeacon of Armagh. It was to set up a committee whose task would be to consider whether it would be desirable to divide the present dioceses of Down, Connor and Dromore, and if desirable to report how such a project could be implemented.

This was the beginning of conversations and negotiations which continued intermittently with the pros and cons debating costs and consequences. Coincidentally two of the clergy in the NO camp, against the division of the dioceses, were Cyril Elliott and W H Good. One was to be elected Bishop of Connor at a later date and the other was a candidate for the vacancy in Down and Dromore on the resignation of W S Kerr. In the many debates on the subject Kerr is mentioned as a frequent contributor. There was real and recognisable movement in the episcopate of JF MacNeice. When he announced his retirement from the See to take effect on 9 April 1942 - he died four days later - attempt was made to bring about a decision to divide the dioceses and a committee was constituted, six representing the Representative Church Body and six the dioceses, and asked to examine that feasibility. The proposal was carried and a committee appointed. It included King

Irwin and it reported to General Synod 1926 that it had consulted with the bishop, Charles Grierson, sought local opinion and had conversations with the Diocesan Council. It concluded that a strong case had been made for a division of the diocese and the suggestion was that it be of Connor from Down and Dromore. The contention was that the parishes in the dioceses would benefit so much that that would outweigh any financial sacrifice.

In advance of the report to General Synod the Diocesan Synod at a meeting on 3 November:

1. Approves of the principle of dividing .the diocese into two.

2. Considers that the best plan of division, would be the separation of the diocese of Connor from those of Down and Dromore.

3. Undertakes to co-operate with the General Synod in financing this division if the General Synod makes proposals that are possible of acceptance in view of the very heavy financial commitments of the diocese.

4. Authorises the Council to consult with the General Synod Committee on the matter.

The financial commitments of the diocese were to be a recurring theme in the negotiations. They were so daunting it was crucial that the General Synod donate a substantial sum to the scheme. The synod of the diocese appended its proposals on the financial arrangements - especially stipends and housing - which would be necessary before the project could proceed. The detail of the statement is such that the influence of financial experts is clearly to be seen. After the General Synod had accepted the report of its committee on the division of the three dioceses the Diocesan Synod on 2nd November 1926 heard from its Council that a committee it had appointed had produced a finding that caused it to conclude:

> "that while reluctant to do anything that might prejudice the successful inauguration and ultimate adoption of such a scheme, yet on financial grounds it would be altogether inopportune at the present time to attempt to attract the monetary support necessary for immediate action. It is hoped, however, that in course of time conditions may improve, when further consideration can be given to providing the means of rendering, the scheme possible."

The General Synod Committee received this decision with "unfeigned regret" and discharged itself at the meeting in 1927. In spite of the situation that had arisen the General Synod showed its practical concern for the problems in Belfast with large contributions towards church extension. The matter was raised again in the General Synod of 1930 but time prevented pursuance of it. However a letter from C K Irwin dated 20th June, to Mr Moore, diocesan secretary, was to move things on again. Irwin, a tenacious advocate of division, laid out the proposals of a Representative Church Body sub-committee of which he was a member. It repeated the suggestion for the division made by the General Synod Committee and asked for a response on finance for such a division, and any other views on the subject, by 10th October. The Council referred the letter to committee representative of the three dioceses. It recommended that

THE RIGHT REV. W. S. KERR. D.D.
RECTOR 1911-1915
LORD BISHOP OF DOWN, 1950

the Council advise the Diocesan Synod to agree to the division of the dioceses as per the Resolution of the RCB, 18th June 1930. But at the meeting of the synod, 28-29th October 1930, when the proposal for division was put, an amendment regretting that in the prevailing conditions "it cannot approve of the scheme put forward by the Council" was carried, clergy 117, lay 76: against clergy 66, lay 122. A resolution was adopted, without dissent, on the motion of the Revs James Quinn and WS Kerr, asking for an extension of time for a consideration of the subject. It proposed a committee be appointed to confer with the RCB and to report to a Diocesan Synod to be called "as early as conveniently possible." The committee of 20 was appointed and the result of their work was the presentation of a majority resolution, 10-8, in favour of the division. There was the request that the bishop summon a Special Meeting of the Diocesan Synod for 3 February 1931. The committee report and resolution had a long dissentient statement signed by 10 of its 19 members. They claimed that the report did not reflect accurately the view of the committee, for two members opposed to the resolution were unavoidably absent and Lord Cushendun had not been present at any of its meetings. At the February meeting, the lack of unanimity showed when those against the new bishopric argued their case with facts and figures which applied not only to the church in the North but to the Church of Ireland as a whole. The dissentient statement had two signatures that of R C H G Elliott, St Patrick's, Ballymacarrett and W H Good, St Mary's, Belfast. The first was to become a Bishop of Connor and the other a candidate for the See of Down and Dromore on the resignation of Bishop Kerr.

In the Special Synod the amendment to the proposal to divide was carried, clerical 116, lay 130; against 57 and 73. Later in the year the General Synod heard the; RCB report which reiterated its opinion that division was the way forward. While it regretted the Down, Connor and Dromore decision, it favoured further assistance to the needy Belfast area. It added the observation that the proposition for the formation of a new bishopric had come, ·not from the diocese but from the church at the centre.

When Bishop Grierson retired in 1934, J F MacNeice was elected to succeed him. 'No move was made to change the situation in his episcopate. On 9th April 1942 MacNeice intimated his intention to resign. He died four days later. At the General Synod of May 1942 a Bill was moved by Judge Thompson that was intended to implement the proposed division of 1925. The Bill was passed, as was a resolution calling for a committee of 12, six nominated by the RCB and six by the Diocesan Council of Down, Connor and Dromore to consider how the problems of the diocese could be resolved. If there could not be agreement on the matter the committee was requested to report on the desirability of planning for an Assistant Bishop to the Diocesan Bishop pending a permanent solution. The Primate presided at the Diocesan Synod called to elect a bishop. It failed to elect and the House of Bishops appointed the Bishop of Limerick, C K Irwin, to the See. He was enthroned in St Anne's Cathedral, Belfast, on 2nd September but declined to be enthroned in the other cathedrals of the United Diocese saying that he had already been enthroned twice, and that was enough for any man. The committee produced a detailed report on all that was involved in a change of diocesan structures. It found that financial considerations affected the thinking of many who were asked to express an opinion. It reported to the RCB on 17th February 1943 that it was unable to make practical recommendations on the division of the dioceses until it knew what monies would be available from central funds to ensure the stipends of the two bishops. The RCB on that date adopted the report of its Finance Committee which detailed the measures to be taken to meet the need entailed in the division of the dioceses. St Anne's Cathedral and its role in a changed diocesan structure had to be clarified. The committee had done its job, and its report met with the approval of the 1943 General Synod. At the special Diocesan Synod on 12th October 1943, to consider the proposal to divide the dioceses, T N D C Salmon and John Barry, on behalf of the junior clergy, disclaimed any opposition to the proposal. The motion was carried on a show of hands. The second special Diocesan Synod of 26th April 1944 was convened to consider Bills for the Division of Down, Connor and Dromore. The Bill to divide had its first and second readings on 9th May and after amendments suggested by Diocesan Synod, had its third reading on 11th May 1944 and became law.

Three matters had to be decided:
1.The Bishop was to choose by 1st November 1944 which diocese he wanted to retain.
2. The RCB was to approve an apportionment scheme and specify
when it would take effect.

3. The whole scheme was to come into operation on an "appointed day" which was to be not later than 1 January 1945.

The Diocesan Synod was to frame and submit a scheme as soon as may be after passing of the Statute. The appointed days suggested by the Diocesan Synod to the RCB
were:
> (a) 1 November 1944 for the provisions with respect to the election of a Bishop to fill the vacancy.
> (b) 1 January 1945 for all other provisions so far not then in force.

These were accepted by the RCB 18th October, 1944. Bishop King Irwin chose the Diocese of Connor and on 8th November 1944. The Dean of Belfast, William Shaw Kerr, was elected Bishop of Down and· Dromore and the division of the dioceses became effective on 1st January 1945.

Educationalist
WS Kerr was deeply involved in the Northern Ireland controversy over religious education which began shortly after the setting up of the state. The controversy was occasioned when the Minister of Education, Lord Londonderry, set out to establish a new primary school system. He had consultations with all the interested parties, and with the churches, for education in Ireland generally had been under church auspices.
The Roman Catholic Church refused to co-operate Cardinal Michael Logue rejected a request from

Londonderry of 29th August 1921 to nominate members for a proposed commission on education because he feared an attack on Roman Catholic schools. In September 1921 a committee of enquiry into education was set up with Robert Lynn MP, and editor of "The Northern Whig" in the chair. Of the 22 members, only one was a Roman Catholic, for the Catholic Church refused representation on it. He was Andrew Bonaparte Wyse whose transfer from the Dublin Government was regarded as a coup for Londonderry for he was respected as the most able and experienced civil servant in, educational affairs. In October 1921 the Catholic school managers met in Dublin and issued a clear warning:

> "…in view of pending changes in Irish education, we wish to assert the great fundamental principle that the only satisfactory system of education for Catholics is one wherein Catholic children are taught in Catholic schools by Catholic teachers under Catholic auspices."

Donald Hermon Akenson in his *Education and Enmity: The Control of Schooling in Northern Ireland, 1920-50* makes this judgement:

> "The refusal of the Catholic religious authorities to exert their influence upon the Lynn Committee and subsequently upon the Londonderry Act was especially unfortunate because despite the civil war which was raging in Northern Ireland the Unionist Government was making a determined effort to govern in a non-sectarian manner, an attempt which was abandoned in mid 1920s."

Londonderry refused to accept the Lynn Committee recommendations on religious education, for he argued that they would have created two denominational systems, separate and unequal. He wanted to be fair to the Catholics, for in a vague and undefined way he was an ecumenist. He spoke of schools where children of different faiths studied and played together. He was not a secularist for he was determined that moral instruction would be associated with secular instruction. His thinking was in line with the Education Act (Northern Ireland) which received the Royal Assent on 22nd June 1921. It stipulated that religious education would be a voluntary appendage to a secular school system. There was strong opposition to this valuation of religious education from both Protestants and Catholics. The Roman Church wanted no part of such a system arguing that the teaching of the Christian faith must permeate every facet of education. The Protestant Churches would only consider the new approach if there was compulsory Bible teaching and teachers of an acceptable denomination appointed to their schools. Londonderry was troubled for he believed that all quarrels between Catholics and Protestants arose out of the teaching of the Bible. The Education Act was regarded as a betrayal by the Protestant Churches who had believed that their interests were secured in the Government of Ireland Act 1920. The Presbyterian Church and the Church of Ireland met in a delegates' conference, to be joined later by the Methodist Church, and forwarded a resolution to the Prime Minister on 31st July 1923. It was ignored and the Government found itself in what was to be a long acrimonious controversy with the churches and the Orange Institution which had set up a special committee to monitor the debate. It became clear that Londonderry defined religious education as instruction in Civics and Ethics. Dr Strahan, a former moderator, castigated Londonderry for saying that the Bible must be seen as a denominational book. The Minister of Education was faced with the dilemma that while the Protestant Churches regarded the Bible as their authority for faith and practice, the Catholic Church gave equal credence to tradition and the writings of the early fathers of the Church. The leaders of the Protestant campaign against the Education Act 1923 were the Revs William Corkey, Presbyterian, James Quinn, Church of Ireland, and W.H.Smyth, Methodist. The Protestant position was spelled out by WS Kerr in a pamphlet, "The Case Against the Education Act." It was written on behalf of the United Education Committee of which the three clerics were often belligerent spokesmen. The opposition to the Government's educational policy became so intense that the Prime Minister found himself confronted - as was evidenced at a Mass Meeting of 5th March 1923 in the Assembly Hall, Belfast - by a platform which included the moderator, leading churchmen, among them W S Kerr and Sir Joseph Davison, the Grand Master of Belfast Orangemen. Craig's fear of pressure on his party politicians caused him to capitulate and to offer an amending Bill in Parliament. Londonderry who was out of the country at the time was not party to the agreement reached by the UEC and the Orangemen. The Education Amending Act was passed on 13th March 1925. While it met some of the demands of the churches, it proved to be the source of contention between Corkey and Londonderry who had their different interpretations of it. The hopes for a settlement were dashed when on 24th

April the UEC asked the Ministry of Education to approve two conditions in the deeds of transfer of former voluntary schools (ie. Protestant schools) and got the reply that under the Government of Ireland Act they would be illegal. They were:

1. That religious instruction was to be given by the teaching staff on a programme approved by the persons or body transferring the school.

2. That if someone offensive religiously to the transferring body were appointed as a teacher the transferors had the right to resume control of the school.

The ministerial objection to Protestant schools getting financial help if they had denominational teaching was a contradiction of the attitude to Catholic schools which were wholly denominational and in receipt of large sums of money. A concordat between Londonderry and the UEC, 22-26 June, was published. The terms as summarised were -

"First, in the future local education authorities were empowered to require that 'a programme of simple Bible instruction' be given in provided or transferred schools in the period set apart for religious instruction. Secondly, this simple Bible instruction, although given during the hours set apart for religious instruction, was not to include denominational dogmas or catechetical points. In other words, it was tacitly understood that the simple Bible reading was to be Protestant in nature but not distinctive of any Protestant denomination. Thirdly, the daily period specified on the timetable for the Bible instruction was not to be included within the hours of compulsory attendance by the children. Given this point the fourth part of the agreement was crucial: teachers were to be compelled to give such simple Bible instruction as part of their required educational duties. The fifth point was that the teachers were not compelled to give denominational instruction if the school managers chose to use the religious time slot for specific denomination teaching instead of general Protestant instruction."

The place and power of the Protestant clergy had been demonstrated in the educational controversy. Akenson said,

"Before partition, the Protestant Ulsterman had often denounced the Catholic 'priest in politics' but no· band, of Catholic priests in the former United Ireland had engaged in politics with the energy and efficiency of the Protestant clerics who led the United Education Committee of the Protestant Churches."

Perhaps they needed to be as militant as they were for there were to be many questionings of Government policy on religious education in the years to come. Delegation after delegation met with the Prime Ministers and the Ministers of Education to enter into more negotiations, to be more annoyed and to suffer more misunderstanding. When comparisons were made with the treatment of Catholics in education the Protestants were seen to be the losers. Unfair treatment was a main grievance and especially in, the training of teachers. A promise backed by Craig that the anomaly, a Catholic Training College and no Protestant one would be removed had not been honoured. The case for a Protestant Training College had been made when the Roman Catholic Church built its college in Belfast at a cost to the public purse of £25,000 and over which it had complete control. When the Stranmillis Training College was founded, William Shaw Kerr was appointed to the management committee in mid July 1933. The antagonism between Government and churches continued until the crucial debates on the Education Act 1947 helped to resolve many of the differences between them. The controversy was of such importance that it deserved better than the often intemperate attacks and counterattacks from participants in that it marks a chapter in Northern Ireland history which should be read and from which much can be learned for education remains the cause of constant concern and controversy here.

Ecumenist

An ecumenical enthusiasm of WS Kerr was for a Church of Ireland agreement with the Old Catholics. He managed to get the General Synod to accept his motion to effect that end. Archbishop J.A.F.Gregg told C Beaufort Moss after the synod that he thought the decision was premature but that Bishop Kerr had pushed it through. Gregg, who had more sympathy with Eastern Orthodoxy, may have felt that the Old Catholics had more to unlearn doctrinally than the Orthodox. N D Emerson who had 'blamed the bishops, Gregg mainly, for the Church's refusal to enter into communion with the Old Catholics used a clerical meeting at which the speaker was RR Hartford, the secretary of the Church

Unity Committee to make his point. Hartford's theme had been the Old Catholics and he was asked to take up the matter with Gregg. The Primate acknowledged that they were cowardly in not doing anything in the matter. Emerson explained, "A Bill came before the General Synod proposed by Bishop Kerr and seconded by me. It was carried almost unanimously."

This ecumenical disagreement between Gregg and Kerr was of much less consequence than the earlier one on inter-church relations when Gregg was Archbishop of Dublin and Kerr was Dean of Belfast. In the 1930s with growing dissention among the three churches Roman, Anglican and Presbyterian - churchmen in the northern Province were moving in favour of reconciling Anglicans and Presbyterians. The Primate C F D'Arcy, encouraged those who felt that a new relationship was desirable. In his presidential address at General Synod 1934 on Christian Reunion he said,

> "There are now movements which simply ignore the divisions of the churches, finding that human souls can attain the beatific vision, and realise the power of Christ to change the life of man, without any reference whatever to the denomination to which the individual belongs. For us, as for all who belong to the Anglican Communion, the APPEAL TO ALL CHRISTIAN PEOPLE issued by the Lambeth Conference of 1920 is the natural starting point for thought on the subject."

The Archbishop of Dublin, Gregg, did not share the Primate's views and made his position clear on 23rd

October 1934 at his synod when he questioned the validity of non-episcopal ordinations. He quoted the Ordinal of 1549, "From the Apostles time there have been three Orders of Ministers in Christ's Church - bishops, priests and deacons and that no man be admitted -thereto unless by Episcopal consecration or ordination." Gregg argued that the Ordinal was reaffirming principles which had governed the Universal Church from the earliest times. He described the reasoning behind the 1920 Lambeth Conference's "Appeal to All Christian People" which aimed at piercing the hitherto impregnable walls dividing the separated communion of Christians.

He said,

> "The bishops reaffirmed the powerful basis of the approach to Home Reunion laid down by. the Lambeth Conference of 1888 (commonly called the Lambeth Quadrilateral) consisting of the acceptance of the Holy Scriptures, the Apostles and Nicene Creeds, the two great Sacraments of the Gospel and the historic episcopate. We do not deny the spiritual reality of the non Episcopal ministries. We thankfully acknowledge that they have been manifestly blessed by the Holy Ghost. But we submit that both the history of the past and the experience of the present justify the claims that such a ministry of the whole body can rest only upon the episcopate."

Kerr did not share this interpretation of the Anglican position as from the Lambeth Conference of 1920. He brought the matter to a head in a proposition to the General Synod in May 1935 when he moved:

"That in accordance with the resolution passed by the Joint Committee of the Church of Ireland and the Presbyterian Church in Ireland on Reunion on January 29 1934, the General Synod of the Church of Ireland declare that: Without prejudice to the convictions held by either church as to the preferable forms and methods of administering the Rite of Ordination and the Sacraments of the Church, and without prejudice to any future arrangements that may be mutually agreed upon: The Church of Ireland fully and freely recognises, as a basis for further progress towards union, the -validity, efficacy and spiritual reality of both Ordination and Sacraments as administered by the Presbyterian Church."

There was an interruption of the proceedings when the Archbishop of Dublin questioned procedures and by a ruling of Judge Best, the Primate's assessor, Gregg was bested. Kerr went on with his speech, "It should not be necessary to emphasise that there was no question before them concerning the episcopal constitution of the Church... to each and all of them episcopacy was one of the fundamental conditions of reunion... What the resolution did involve was simply the recognition of their Presbyterian brethren, when they came to the Table of the Lord in obedience to His command, received the fullness of His sacramental blessing. Could that be doubted for one moment? Remember, it was this synod that initiated the conferences. So, as a condition of further negotiation, it was required that each church accept definitely and unmistakably the full authenticity of the others Orders and Sacraments. We can confer on no other basis... Let it be clearly understood that this resolution goes not a whit beyond the Appeal To All Christian People issued by the bishops of the Anglican Communion in 1920. The united episcopate explicitly acknowledges the spiritual reality of these ministries and that they are 'manifestly blessed and owned by the Holy Spirit as an effective means of grace.' That was reaffirmed by the Lambeth Conference of 1930. That is all we ask this synod to agree to."

He pointed out in the Articles of Religion, and also in the Preface of the Ordinal, two things are made clear; one, that the Church ensures for itself an episcopal constitution; the other, that it carefully refrains from specifying that episcopacy is essential to the nature of the Church. And the Nineteenth Article defines the visible church without reference to episcopacy. Kerr concluded:

"We are asked to come into line with the Lambeth bishops and declare our recognition of the reality - the validity – of non-episcopal ministries. A refusal - which God forbid means that we stamp these ministries as unreal and delusive... Does not the present crisis admonish us to heal our divisions, to rise above unnecessary theological feuds, to stand for the great essentials which alone can save the faith? It is 15 years since the Lambeth bishops "warned us that the faith cannot be adequately apprehended, and the battle of the Kingdom cannot worthily be fought, while the body is divided. Each succeeding year makes that message more impressive. I beseech you to take away a stumbling block in the road to a new realisation of unity, fellowship and power."

While Kerr's speech received prolonged applause and-the backing of some fine speakers in a lively debate it was Gregg who had the last word when he moved an amendment:

"The synod has considered the report of the Joint Committee presented to the General Synod, 1934, 'and has noted its contents. It has also had opportunity to consider the report of the Committee appointed by the Archbishop of Canterbury to confer with representatives of the Church of Scotland. It has also learned the condition prescribed by the General Assembly of 6 June 1934 for the Representatives of the Assembly to engage in further discussion on the subject of reunion in Ireland with Representatives of the General Synod. It recognises with regret, that approach to the question of reunion in Ireland along the lines of the 'Appeal To All Christian People', Lambeth 1920, or the Lambeth Resolution of 1930, offers no present prospect of success, and that further consideration of this important question must, accordingly, be deferred until more promising methods' of approach present themselves."

He said the amendment would turn aside a direct vote on the validity of another Church's Orders and Sacraments.

"The resolution was in direct opposition to the Lambeth principle, which said, 'Ask no question of the other Church. Give what you have, and take what they have.' We have been separated from the Presbyterian Church for 400 years, and now are proposing to give away the point which has been at issue for that period."

The Primate C F D'Arcy who spoke from the floor of the house favoured the motion but added that he would rather that Gregg's amendment were passed than that the proposal be rejected. He said,

> "Speaking of the matter from the higher side, apart from the fighting about words, the Presbyterian Church is one of the most splendid Churches in the world. From its theologians he had learnt much. He would say without fear of contradiction that in the realm of philosophical theology the Presbyterian Church stood at the head of the whole Christian world. To be in association with that Church was something for which he would thank God."

Kerr said that if the amendment was carried it would be the end of all efforts for reunion. The amendment was carried by a large majority. The original motion received only a few votes. George Seaver in his *John Allen Fitzgerald Gregg, Archbishop* said of the episode, Gregg "had saved the Church of Ireland from what would have been a perilous lapse into latitudinarianism". The Concise Oxford Dictionary of the Christian Church defines the word as - "a term applied approbiously in the 17th century, to the outlook of Anglican divines who continued within the Church of England but attached relatively little importance to matters of dogmatic truth, ecclesiastical organisation, and liturgical practice." There are those in these more ecumenical days who deplore the rehashing of the divisive attitudes and events of the past. But to know history when it is necessary to understand reasons why the churches' remain separate and distinct in their identities is essential to anyone who deplores the disunity of Irish Christendom.

It is necessary for us to look back, sometimes with pleasure and thanksgiving for what our forefathers have done for us; and with anger and regret that they were guilty of sins against Christ and Christianity which are perpetuated in our own unhappy divisions. To Kerr and those like him who tried to give a fair and balanced view of church history we should feel deeply indebted. WS Kerr, to his credit, while showing pride in his Anglicanism was always a supporter of inter-church relations. He was more sensitive to the aims and aspirations of churchmen of other traditions than most of the leaders and people of his own church. It can be no more than an exercise in conjecture as to whether his inter-church emphases would have made much difference to religion in Ireland. Would the apparently indelible denominationalism have been so affected that by now we would have a federated church with its ministries, forms and ceremonies enriched by the gifts of each member church? If that can never be a reality it must have been possible to move much more in that direction to make denominational competition as unnecessary as it is wasteful of the resources of the churches and a weakening of their witness to Christ in the world. It takes little imagination to picture the greater efficiency and effectiveness of a united, consolidated

Christian witness of churches released from the ties of introverted denominationalism.

The duplication of resources is an indictment on the churches for their selfishness and self-interestedness. The situation is worsened by the fact that doctrinally the Reformed Churches are so agreed that controversies do not occur and liturgical differences are less marked. What remains are historical attitudes with religious and political undertones and they are the regulatory factors in inter-church associations. We should deplore this situation as it is most likely that WS Kerr worried about it in his day when antipathies were stronger and much more public than they are today. We should feel the pressures of galloping secularism.

Polemicist

"Kerr's writings, though mainly historical, had a content of theological thinking which explained the attitudes of people and the events which were to be seen in a religious context. A researcher for truth and an uncoverer of error, he wrote with commendable simplicity and sensitivity."

While he was the author of several learned papers, a contributor to journals and· newspapers, his literary reputation rests on four major works - *The Independence of the Celtic Church in Ireland*, (1931); *Walker of Derry*, (1938); *Who Persecuted: Episcopalian and, Presbyterian in Ulster*, (1947); and *A Handbook on the Papacy*, (1950). Mainly historical the works have a content of theological thinking which explains the attitudes of people, and the events which must be seen in a religious context. Kerr's object in writing is to defend his Church of Ireland against the false claims and unfair charges of other churches against it. He is a searcher after truth and an uncoverer of error; a meticulous researcher. His skill as a writer showed in the clarity, simplicity and sensitivity of his writing. He prepared his material as would a lawyer whose case must not be lost for lack of evidence to clear his client of the charges made against him. In his foreword to *The Independence of the Celtic Church* H J Lawlor, Dean of St Patrick's Cathedral, Dublin, describes the book, and Kerr, when he says:

> "I believe that his argument is sound. Those who are inclined to follow the many respectable historians who take a different view, should read the excellent chapter entitled Fictions and Forgeries."

Kerr's intention was to give an honest unembroidered reading of the beginnings of Irish Church History. He takes to task those Roman Catholic scholars whom he claims have misused history by accepting and incorporating" in their writings fables, often ridiculous stories of Patrick, the early Irish saints and miraculous healings, instantaneous and incredible. In his Author's Preface the then Archdeacon of Dromore asks the question "was the ancient Celtic Church independent and self governing?" He goes on to describe the claims of the Church of Rome to be the one and only true church of Jesus Christ and quotes in a footnote the Bull Unum Sanctum of Pope Boniface, VIII:

> "We declare, say, define and pronounce that it is entirely necessary for salvation for every creature to be subject to the Roman Pontiff."

Kerr's thesis was to show that this claim of sovereignty and supremacy was not recognised by the Celtic Church, and British Christians, who were determinedly independent. They resisted Roman Church pressures, often at great cost to themselves. He makes two points, one, originally Roman bishops "did not demand the subjection of other churches one the dogmatic grounds that have since been promulgated?"

Secondly, there was a recognition of the importance of the Church in Rome placed strategically as it was in the capital of the Roman Empire. Kerr begins his study with St Patrick – there is a note on Celtic Christians before Patrick - and his writings which give no credence to claim that, "he was subject to the Pope as Vicar of Christ and Head of the whole Church and Father and Teacher of all Christians." Kerr's analytical examination of the Patrician literature causes him to conclude that:

> "Patrick neither obtained nor recognised as supreme the sanction of the Roman Pontiff for his work in Ireland."

The biographical references in Patrick's writings are used as insights into the character and conduct of the man. The listing and evaluation of the early biographies of St Patrick is useful to an understanding of his motivations and aims and to show how garbled were the accounts of his life; the fictionalising of his experiences and the events in which he participated. Mostly these were originally intended to eulogise Patrick but it is apparent that the material was altered and adapted to give it a Roman slant. The fabrications and dishonesty of several writers cause Kerr to quote with approval Archbishop Healy's rule:

"Every statement - in any life of St Patrick, ancient or modern, clearly inconsistent with the tenor of these documents (St Patrick's Confession and Epistle) must be rejected without hesitation."

Kerr, using much source material, demonstrates that the independence from Rome of the Celtic Church showed so clearly that it should not be questioned. Similarly he demonstrates that for centuries there was the struggle with Rome and the determination of Irish, and the old British, Christians, in communion with· them, to hold their own traditional customs and practices. This even when Rome was more rational and realistic in its thinking as instanced in the dating of Easter. The book has very brief profiles of Columbanus, Augustine (of Canterbury), Laurentius and Theodore in England and their relations with the Celtic Church, never cordial but sometimes ambiguous. And there was Wilfrid, Bishop of Ripon, enigmatic and forcible, the pro-Roman antagonist of Celtic Christianity who rose and fell by the favour and disfavour of his royal patron Alfrid. Featured is the Synod of Whitby 664 and its pivotal place in Roman/Celtic relations at which Wilfrid as the main advocate for Romanism was opposed by Bishop Colman and Hilda, Abbess of Whitby. The royal decision after the pleas were heard was that there should 'be obedience to St Peter the doorkeeper. The decision by King Oswy came from the threat, "lest when I come to the gates of the Kingdom of Heaven there should be none to open them he being my adversary who is proved to have the keys." Kerr adds: "The doom of the Celtic Church in Britain was pronounced. Rome had vanquished Iona in England."

The outcome was the resignation of Colman from his bishopric and with his colleagues at Lindisfarne, Irish monks and English disciples, he left Britain for exile at Iona and then to lnishbofin, a little island off the coast of Mayo, the "Island of the White Cow". 'The struggle with Rome in Ireland is not well chronicled for it had no Venerable Bede, but Kerr traces a way through the available data to provide an interesting explanation of the course of events. These were affected especially in Ulster by the close connection with Iona and Scotland where resistance to Rome was strongest. Iona succumbed to Ronlan Pressure in 772 but Dowden in his *Celtic Church in Scotland* states that, "the Columban monks in Pictland adhered to the old ways after lona abandoned them." In the life of St Columba "there is not one trace of the Pope or the slightest acknowledgment of his claims." While St Columbanus makes many mentions of the Pope and letters to Popes, there is no sign of any commitment to Rome. On the contrary the claims of Rome are often rejected and warnings given that pressure must not be applied to him, and those for whom he spoke. Kerr shows that it is to the .discredit of Roman historians like Lanigan, Crew and Brennan that they deliberately missed quotes from Columbanus. The tricks of some historians were such that what they wrote reads like the work of a novelist specialising in mysteries with strong psychological undertones. The Roman Catholic take-over in Ireland is described with the association of church and crown which brought that about. The entry came via the Danes Professor G T Stokes explains:

"The Danes formed one principal channel through which the Papal See renewed and accomplished its designs upon the independence of the Irish Church in the course of the eleventh and twelfth centuries. (*Ireland and the Celtic Church*, p277) They possessed three cities Dublin, Waterford and Limerick and by them contributed to the Romanizing of the Celtic Church. The main character in the drama was Turlough, King of Ireland, and grandson of Brian Boru, who gave consent to Roman infiltration into the Irish Church life. Pope Gregory VII in a letter to Turlough claimed absolute sovereignty over the church in Ireland, one never before heard in Ireland, that Christ had placed Holy Church above all the Kingdoms of the earth, and putting into subjection unto her principalities and powers and all that seems possessed of dignity or grandeur in the world, in fulfilment of the prophecy of Isaiah: They that spake against Thee shall come to Thee and bow themselves down to the soles of Thy feet."

The submission was that the Pope, as the Vicar of Christ was owed a debt of obedience as well as reverence. The genuineness of the letter has been questioned but if the communication is genuine it is the first claim of full lordship over Ireland. Kerr concludes:

"The Church of Ireland had flourished for over six hundred years of her existence without hearing of or yielding such subjection. Her days of freedom were nearly over and with them her days of glory."

The subjection to Rome is dated to the twelfth century. Two bishops Gilbert of Limerick, first Papal Legate in Ireland, and Malachy, Down and Connor, later

Archbishop of Armagh, played large parts in the absorption of the Church of Ireland by the Church of Rome. The Synod of Rathbreasil in 1110 mapped out 24 territorial dioceses. 12 North and 12 South, to have Ireland conform to the Roman hierarchical system and "gave to Ireland a paper constitution of the approved Roman and Catholic type." The Synod of Kells underlined the lordship of the Pope on the Irish Church and by enactments reorganised it into four Archiepiscopal provinces and fixed the number and boundaries of dioceses. Soon the secular freedom of Ireland was to go, too, when twenty years after the Synod of Kells Pope Adrian IV by Papal Bull invited King Henry II of England to take over Ireland. Kerr quotes Lanigan:

> "Adrian's Bull is of so unwarrantable and unjustifiable a nature that some writers could not bring themselves to believe that he issued it, and have endeavoured to prove it a forgery; but their efforts are of no avail, and never did there exist a more real or authentic document."

It was the basis of the Norman conquest of Ireland. The Synod of Cashel 1172 presided over by the Papal Legate, Christian, Bishop of Lismore, was intended to suppress what remained of native church customs. Well organised and manned for that purpose it was most successful for it brought about the enslavement of Irishmen religiously and politically and their degradation as a people. The Statutes of Kilkenny 1367 proscribed all things Irish. Kerr points out:

> "Up to the time of the Norman Conquest we never hear of the Pope appointing a bishop in

Ireland. The Statutes of Kilkenny represent the mind and policy of the church in Ireland when it became fully papal."

He finishes on this note:

"Is the day far off when patriotic Irishmen will unite in a church self-governing, independent, released from foreign jurisdiction, and reviving the freedom and evangelical traditions of the Church of St Patrick?"

Historian

In Kerr's Foreword to his *Walker of Derry* he proposes to do two things:

"to arouse fresh interest in the dauntless heroism of the men who defended the city in 1689. Their faith and spirit should be an abiding inspiration to their descendents; and to vindicate the Rev George Walker who has been repeatedly assailed and the disparagements have been recently revived. The evidence here produced demonstrates how unfounded such aspersions were. Contemporary sources clearly reveal how discreditable they are."

The book was dated to appear in time for the 250th anniversary of the Siege. The retelling of that story, one of the great historical events of Irish and British history, is done with awareness of detail and a sense of the pivotal importance of the event.

Kerr contends that:

"The results of the victory at Derry were of more than national importance. It was not only the liberties of Ireland and Great Britain that were at stake. The schemes of Louis XIV, for the domination of Europe, were defeated on the banks of the Foyle and the Boyne. The heroes of Derry were the champions of mightier issues than they dreamt of. In defending Derry they saved Europe."

He points up who and what are important in the Siege to make the defenders and attackers believable, people free from the glamour, glorification, and vilification, which has been attached to them by people whose romanticism has often hidden the reality of the bravery and self-sacrifice of those within the walls. Kerr managed to chart a course through the heavy undergrowth of Siege material so that we are speedily introduced to those who were the key figures at Derry in 1689. His concentration on them means that the protagonists are identified to take their places in the drama he pictures for us.

The defence of Walker is done with the skill of an advocate determined to prove that his client is innocent of the charges levelled against him. Walker, leader and soldier, was a country rector of Donaghmore, Co Tyrone, from 1674. His father and grandfather were clergymen and successively rectors of Cappagh and Badoney diocese of Derry. The father had had to flee from Ireland to England in the rebellion of 1641 and returned to his livings at the Restoration in 1660. Walker of Derry was probably born in England during his father's exile, perhaps in 1646. Kerr shows that those biographers who date his birth in 1618, to make him 71 at the Siege, were clearly wrong, for in that year his father was a student in Dublin, aged 17. He produces evidence which supports his own dating and the portrait by Sir Geoffrey Kneller on the command of King William III with other portraits and contemporary engravings, show that he is a man in the prime of life. Walker shared the fears of Protestants that there would be a repeat of 1641 and raised a regiment under Lord Charlemont to defend Dungannon. He defended his action:

> "Clergymen are allowed to be capable of the privileges of mankind and of all creatures in the world. They may all defend themselves and there may such necessity lie upon them that it is their duty to do it."

Kerr explains Walker's attitude:

> "He maintained that the man who did not (act in self defence) was guilty of *felo de se*. He thinks the breach of canonical rules is justified by the necessity of his situation."

It was from Dungannon that Walker went for a consultation with the commander-in-chief, Colonel Robert Lundy, the appointee of William III. Lundy, traitor or incompetent, was not easy to categorise. Walker found that the C-in-C was highly regarded as a soldier though he was later to declare Lundy a traitor. He found him lacking in his defence of Dungannon with his refusal to accept that the approaching army of King James threatened their very existence. This attitude compelled Walker and his men to go to Derry to make it the last stand against James. Kerr's judgment on Lundy is of condemnation and the reasons are clearly argued. The joint-governorship of Derry after Lundy's escape from the country, Major Bakerand the Rev George

Walker, was seen as the city's determination to defend itself. Baker was the professional soldier who had proved himself at Carrickfergus and the Break of Dromore. Walker was to inspire the defenders and to administer the affairs of the city. The denigration of Walker - he had earned the highest praise from the defenders, the King, Parliament and the British public - was very much the pursuit of the Rev John Mackenzie, Presbyterian minister, who felt that his fellow Presbyterians had been denied credit for their part in the Siege. Kerr shows that his personal animosity to Walker coloured everything, he said about him. Mackenzie is described as someone who found collegiality in his own denomination very difficult for he had tendency to quarrel. He was so unpopular that at his death he appears to have left the church for there is no record of his passing. Kerr corrected the Presbyterian Witherow who said he died in 1694 and Reid and Killen who agree on 1696 for he is named as having attended the Synod of Ulster in 1697. Kerr does a good job "as council for the 'defence of Walker by examining the evidence against him in detail. It shows that while Mackenzie was a better writer than Walker he used his skill maliciously.

Kerr compared the hurriedly produced Walker *True Account of the Siege of Londonderry* with its weaknesses from the haste to recount at once the happenings in' Derry, with the nine months later Mackenzie, *A Narrative of the Siege of Londonderry or the late Memorable Transactions of that City, faithfully represented to rectify the mistakes and supply the Omissions of Mr Walker's account.* Allowing that Mackenzie's work has much merit as an account of the Siege, Kerr argues that: "He allowed bitterness to obscure his judgment, and lead him to grossly unjust slanders."

The attack on Walker's character and position as governor was answered by an anonymous friend in a pamphlet *Mr John Mackenzie's Narrative of the Siege of Londonderry a false libel: in defence of Dr George Walker written by his friend in his absence.* Mackenzie answered that with *Dr Walker's Invisible Champion Foiled.* The controversy closed with Walker emerging unscathed. The matter would have died there had not the Presbyterian historian, the Rev Dr W.D. KiIlen more than 150 years later revived it by endorsing the charges made against Walker by Mackenzie and adding a few of his own.

Kerr's brief then is to show that Mackenzie, Killen and the other Presbyterian historians who followed his lead, Reid, Milton, Latimer, Witherow and Moody, were not only unjust to Walker but untrue in their treatment of the well documented data on the Siege. Apart from the personal antipathy of Mackenzie for Walker the main charge was that he had failed to give credit to the Presbyterians whose involvement in the Siege was larger than that of the Episcopalians. In their numbers game the Presbyterians were guilty of failing to recognise that the named leaders of the defenders at the Siege were members of the Church of Ireland. The reality was that denominational loyalties were discounted and

"the Church and Kirk did jointly preach and pray In St Columba's Church most lovingly Where Dr Walker to their great content Preached stoutly against a Popish government, Master Mackenzie preached on the same theme And taught the Army to fear Cod's Great Name."

The charges that Walker was never joint-governor, first with Baker and then with Michelburne, that he was dishonest and drunken, were demonstrably false. The premier place that Walker held was evidenced when his name appears first of the signatories to the Siege documents. The attack on Walker as someone who paraded himself as a man of courage belittled his detractors, for he had shown outstanding bravery when he formed his company to defend Dungannon and to take it to Londonderry for its defence. His selection as a commander of a corps of defenders was recognition by his peers of his courage and skill as a soldier. The worst smear of all was to make his death at the Boyne an unnecessary sacrifice by claiming that he had no reason to be there. The truth is that Walker was killed in the company of the Duke of Schomberg, the most ,experienced commander at the Boyne, in the' thick of battle. Kerr's defence of Ezekiel Hopkins, Bishop of Derry, is a necessary contribution to a better understanding of the actions of another much maligned Siege personality. Kerr's intention to make historical writing fair to the history with which it deals is an altogether laudable one. The misuse of history must be condemned so that readers will not be misled to become themselves purveyors of error. Kerr justified himself: "the defence of truth against manifest error is a manifest duty." (Foreword to *A Handbook on the Papacy* p5).

Controversialist

Kerr "never let his bone go with the dog." He was constantly on the defensive when an attack was mounted on his Church of Ireland. The booklet *Who Persecuted:*

Episcopalian and Presbyterian in Ulster (1947) was his response to statements and criticisms made in a radio talk by Dr A McBeath, Professor of Logic and Metaphysics at Queen's University, Belfast and afterwards published in *The Presbyterian Herald* Kerr's rebuttal of the charges made by McBeath, and Presbyterian scholars generally, against Episcopalians is primarily a plea for a proper and unbiased reading of church history. His admittance of wrongs done by Anglicans to Presbyterians is a challenge to them to admit their own intolerance which showed in a ruthless pressure for uniformity to their system of church government. As was his wont he quotes the Presbyterian apologists and argues his case from their own sources to show by questioning their assertions that they are guilty of unfairness, and lacking in honesty, especially in those events where the Presbyterians are the alleged victims. He demonstrates that in the case of the evictions of Presbyterian ministers by Church of Ireland bishops, and Jeremy Taylor particularly. The fact that they were originally the evictors received no mention. The illegitimacy of the Presbyterian ministers' occupancy of Church of Ireland incumbencies is disregarded and sympathy expressed for the legally evicted Presbyterians. The intemperate attacks on the bishops for doing their duty brings no credit on the historians. Kerr deals painstakingly with cases, and quoting personalities and situations, presents a strong defence of what had to happen when ministers used Anglican churches to practice Presbyterianism and denounce the episcopate. The value of the book is in its presentation of the essential background material necessary to a proper understanding of religion in Ireland in the seventeenth century, and as a warning that the demand of uniformity in Christian faith and practice was shared by Anglicans and Presbyterians. Toleration, was at a discount, compulsion to conform to set patterns of Christianity was the besetting sin of the age.

William Shaw Kerr's *A Handbook on the Papacy* is essential reading for anyone who wants to understand the claims the Roman Catholic Church makes for itself and the Protestant response to them. The book is at once a critique of Roman Catholicism and a justification of Reformed Christianity. It deals with Papal claims to Supremacy and Infallibility and the attitude to the Scriptures. It examines the claims by source materials which include the New Testament; the early church fathers Clement, Tertullian, Iranaeus, Cyprian, Firmilian, Hippolytus, and Athansius; the Councils at Arles, Nicaea, Sardica, Constantinople, Ephesus, Chalcedorl, Constance and the first Vatican Council; the Popes Victor, Liberius, Zosimus, Honorius and Gregory the Great. Reference is made to Basil, Augustine, Jerome, and Columbanus. The questions are here, "Was St Peter at Rome?" "Was St Peter Bishop of Rome?" Roman claims and Roman coercion are dealt with in Kerr's concentration on the Inquisition, and the Spanish Inquisition and the Great Schism. There is such an extensive examination of Roman Catholicism that it would be hard to find any omission of personalities and events which are relevant to a study of the subject. The result is a well argued, well documented, painstakingly researched thesis. The book which made an impression on publication appears to be little regarded today and that must be a pity for the better relationships, Romanist and Protestant, must not cause us to conclude that doctrinal, authoritarian and sociological differences, them and us, have been resolved. The tone of Kerr's treatment of the subject is scholarly and analytical without rancour and resentment. His purpose in writing is the conviction that the defence of the truth is an essential pursuit of the historian. He is in the company of those who in every age have found it incumbent on them to defend the faith against Romish errors - Jewell, Cosin, Overall, Laud, Andrewes, Usher, Jeremy Taylor, Bramhall, Barrow, Pusey, Palmet, Whately, Littledale, Salmon, Gore, Bright, Puller, Denny, Hammond and John Allen Fitzgerald Gregg.

The relationships of the churches have changed since Kerr's time. In many places inter-church activities are normal. When causes are of importance to Christian people they support them regardless of denominational affiliation. The antagonisms which were so obvious in the past and .that often culminated in verbal attacks are occasional happenings now. While it can be argued·, and with justification, that while there were other political, economical and sociological reasons for attacks, Roman Catholics/Protestants, there is no denying that the concentration on religious differences was largely responsible for civil unrest, and ,was a major contributor to the perpetuation of divisions which have characterised Ireland for centuries. Because these divisions still exist it may be argued that the way to halt division is to forget the quarrels of the past, whether mental or physical, political or theological and for people to determine to live together without the shackles of the ·past. But to do that would be to ignore the things which remain of the utmost importance, to them, religion and politics. These were and will remain the dividers ill our society, for even though religion is no longer the dominant force here its influence is indelibilised in the lives of our people. Politics by the nature of its, variableness produces aims and aspirations which inevitably separate people from one another. The better way must be for them to know their history, to be aware of their origins and to rationalise their attitudes. To expel ignorance of those from whom we differ and to know what they think, is an essential thing. We should not condemn others for what they believe or be condemned for what we believe. Truth is what matters. To know the truth must be the desire of people; to teach the truth has to be the commitment of the historian. If we accept that premise we are compelled to recognise the value of such a work as *A Handbook on the Papacy* for the pursuit of truth is the task Kerr set himself.

Kerr was an Orangeman and a Grand Chaplain of the Loyal Orange Institution of Ireland. He regarded his membership as important to him and saw Orangeism as a binding force in Protestantism and a defence of it. His influence in the organisation may have been less noticeable than that of several other Orange chaplains, it is hard to believe though that his voice was ever silent when he felt the need to express an opinion give advice or pass judgement in lodge. Kerr was a forceful character who ensured that he was heard when a matter interested him, and there were few subjects on which he had nothing to say. He would have made his contributions intelligibly and sensitively and his brethren would have listened and taken heed to what he said. As a member of the Historical Committee of Grand Lodge when it published *Orangeism in Ireland and throughout the Empire* by R M Sibbett, it is likely he had an input into its production.

My recollections of Bishop Kerr are of a kindly, sympathetic, and encouraging father-in-God; both as a student and curate I found him easy to talk to and willing to give advice when it was sought. His appointment as first Bishop of Down and Dromore was a particularly good one, given his large and varied experiences in the church. Such a man was needed to steer the diocese through the early days of adaptation to changed circumstances. The smoothness of the change owed much to his personality and skill. Robin Eames, as Bishop of Down and
Dromore, said:

> "I think of William Shaw Kerr, who steered Down and Dromore through the immediate post-war years as it became a separate diocese: a man who ordained clergy in numbers which seem so unbelievable in today's world."

There was no CACTM in Kerr's days and decisions on the qualities and qualifications of would-be ordinands had to be made by him alone. There is a collegiality in the House of Bishops today which would hardly have been to the liking of individualists like Kerr and King Irwin, who 'while very different in manner, the brusque Irwin and the easily approachable Kerr, were alike in their determination to make their own decisions. They ensured that what they said and did were consonant with the ethos of the Church of Ireland and not unacceptable to their episcopal colleagues.

There is no point in trying to compare bishops past and present they serve in different worlds but we should remember with gratitude what the Irwins and Kerrs did for the Church of Ireland.